1	2	3	4	5	6	7	8	9	10
11	12	13	14	15	16	17	18	19	20
21	22	23	24	25	26	27	28	29	30
31	32	33	34	35	36	37	38	39	40
41	42	43	44	45	46	47	48	49	50
51	52	53	54	55	56	57	58	59	60
61	62	63	64	65	66	67	68	69	70
71	72	73	74	75	76	77	78	79	80
81	82	83	84	85	86	87	88	89	90
91	92	93	94	95	96	97	98	99	100
101	102	103	104	105	106	107	108	109	110
111	112	113	114	115	116	117	118	119	120
121	122	123	124	125	126	127	128	129	130
131	132	133	134	135	136	137	138	139	140
141	142	143	144	145	146	147	148	149	150
151	152	153	154	155	156	157	158	159	160
161	162	163	164	165	166	167	168	169	170
171	172	173	174	175	176	177	178	179	180
181	182	183	184	185	186	187	188	189	190
191	192	193	194	195	196	197	198	199	200
201	202	203	204	205	206	207	208	209	210
211	212	213	214	215	216	217	218	219	220
221	222	223	224	225	226	227	228	229	230
231	232	233	234	235	236	237	238	239	240
241	242	243	244	245	246	247	248	249	250
251	252	253	254	255	256	257	258	259	260
261	262	263	264	265	266	267	268	269	270
271	272	273	274	275	276	277	278	279	280
281	282	283	284	285	286	287	288	289	290
291	292	293	294	295	296	297	298	299	300
301	302	303	304	305	306	307	308	309	310
311	312	313	314	315	316	317	318	319	320
321	322	323	324	325	326	327	328	329	330
331	332	333	334	335	336	337	338	339	340
341	342	343	344	345	346	347	348	349	350

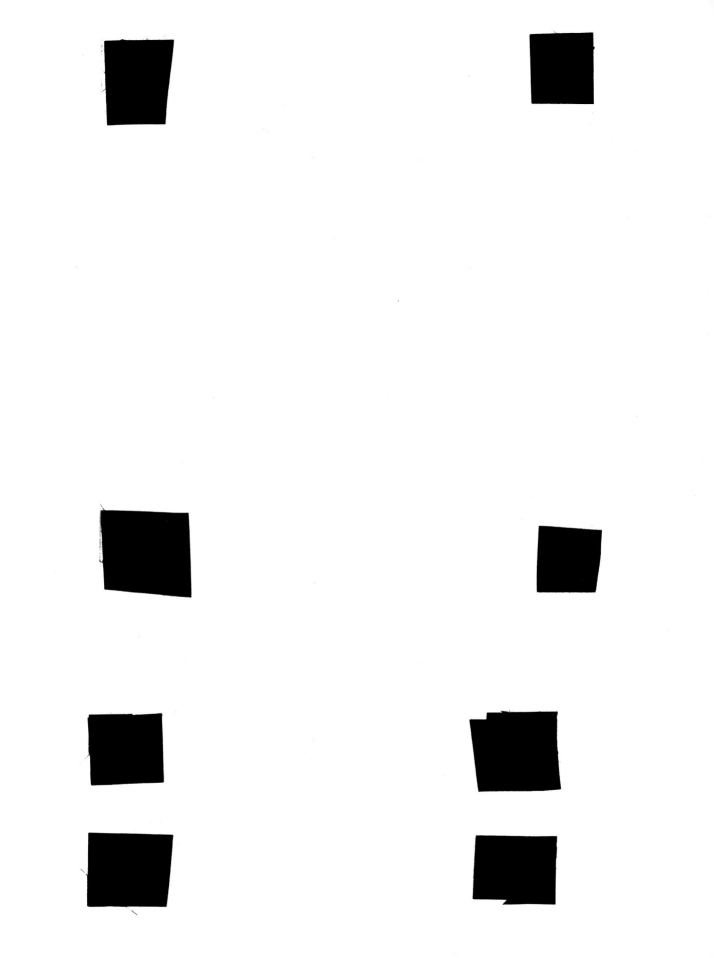

(This is the answer. Turn page for question.)

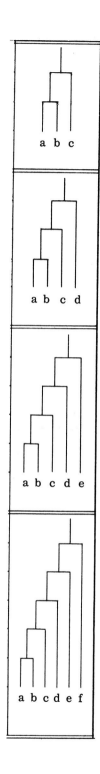

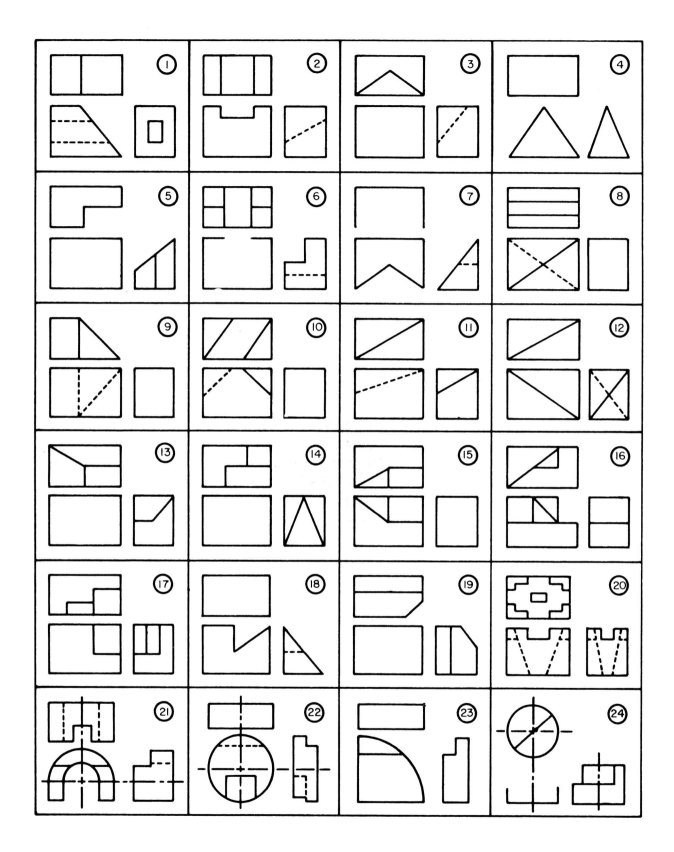

3. A circle.
4. A line.
5. A tiger's nail or claw.
6. A peacock's foot.
7. The jump of a hare.
8. The leaf of a blue lotus.
1. Sounding.
2. Half moon.

drawn diagrams:

I am not entitled to what I have

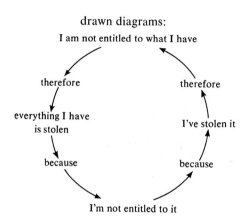

therefore

therefore

everything I have
is stolen

I've stolen it

because

because

I'm not entitled to it

Take that whip out of your hand.
Leg die Peitsche aus der Hand.

I love you most when I watch you eat.
Es macht solchen Spass Dir beim Essen zuzusehen.

$$
\begin{array}{ll}
\mathrm{N} \\
\hline
2 & ++ \\
3 & ++- \\
4 & +++-;\ ++-+ \\
5 & +++-+ \\
7 & +++--+- \\
11 & +++---+--+- \\
13 & ++++--++-+-+ \\
\end{array}
\tag{3}
$$

H

$\mathrm{H^A\ H^B\ H^a\ H^b\ H^2\ H^3}$

$\mathrm{H_A\ H_B\ H_a\ H_b\ H_2\ H_3}$

$\mathrm{H^{\mathit{A}}\ H^{\mathit{B}}\ H^{\mathit{a}}\ H^{\mathit{b}}\ H^{\mathit{2}}\ H^{\mathit{3}}}$

$\mathrm{H_{\mathit{A}}\ H_{\mathit{B}}\ H_{\mathit{a}}\ H_{\mathit{b}}\ H_{\mathit{2}}\ H_{\mathit{3}}}$

$\mathrm{H^{\alpha}\ H^{\beta}\ H^{\lambda}\ H^{\mu}\ H^{\pi}}$

$\mathrm{H_{\alpha}\ H_{\beta}\ H_{\lambda}\ H_{\mu}\ H_{\pi}}$

$\mathrm{H^A\ H^B\ H^a\ H^b\ H^2\ H^3}$

$\mathrm{H_A\ H_A\ H_a\ H_b\ H_2\ H_3}$

$\mathrm{H_{\mathit{A}}\ H_{\mathit{a}}\ H^{\mathit{a}}\ H^{\mathit{b}}}$

$\mathrm{H^1\ H^2\ H^3\ H^4\ H^5}$

$\mathrm{H_1\ H_2\ H_3\ H_4\ H_5}$

$\mathbf{H^1\ H^2\ H^3\ H^4\ H^5}$

$\mathbf{H_1\ H_2\ H_3\ H_4\ H_5}$

We are not trying to you anything...

We only want to

FOR INSTANCE

WHEN THE

FIRST LINES

3---Don't speak to me in obscurities

4---Let's forget we're brothers

5---There's a light across the valley

6---I've been raised

7---There are two porches on the minds

8---Periods and mailboxes

9---It's easy to let go

10--Prejudice goes deeper

11--Place a child on the countryside

12--This is a stick-up, Buddy

13--I cried out in the night

14--I fired once and dropped my gun

15--Kill me if you can

16--Center lines on roads, I dreamed

17--What fear is this

18--Wisdom comes in bits and pieces

19--Pebble dropped in pond

20--A tree in the forest is not so great

21--There's an apple

22--Danger lurks within the thought

23--I don't like you anymore

24--My flag is not a banner

25--You stand alone

26--Grammar never taught me

27--From without

28--Cheapest ads on billboards

29--Fifty thousand shrines to God

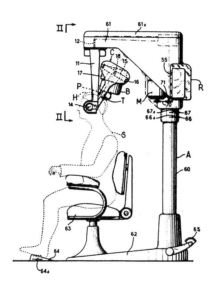

—Think Zinc

TO
NE
US

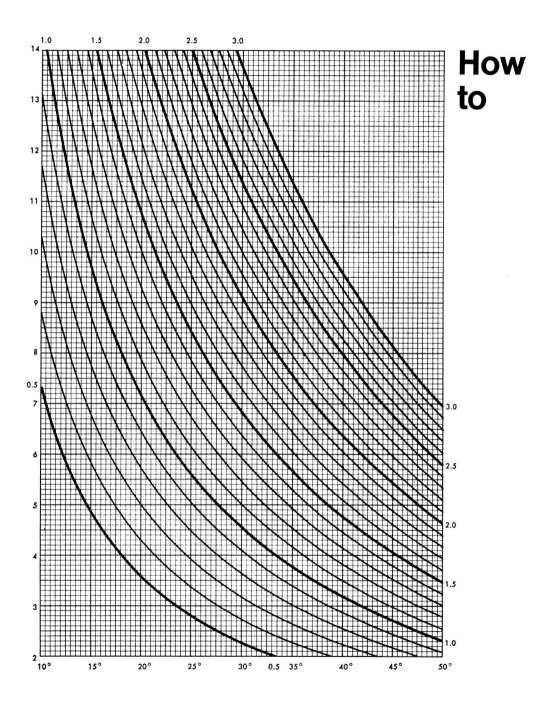

How
to

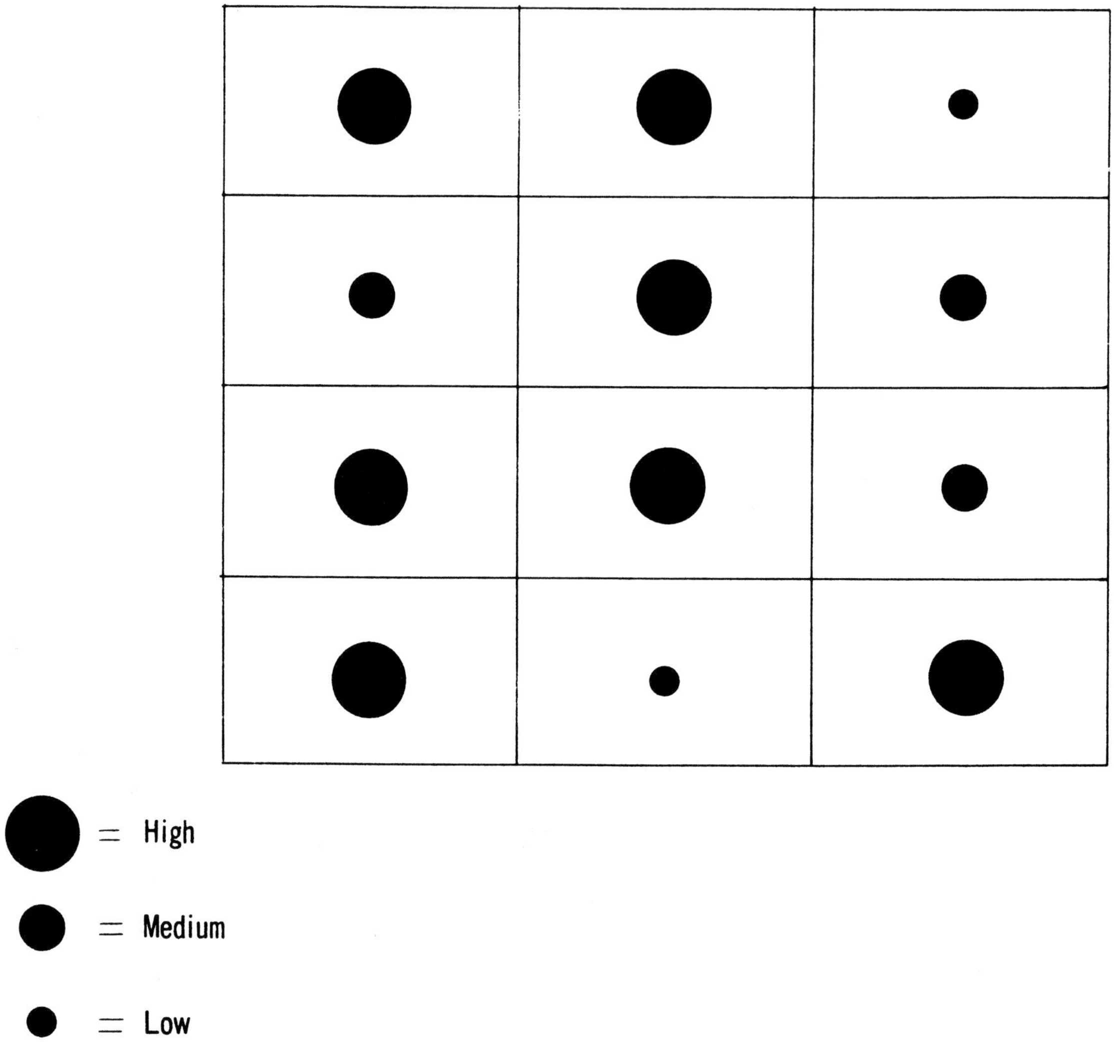

●   = High

●   = Medium

●   = Low

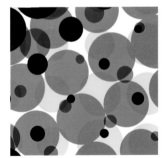

THE WILCO BOOK

by Wilco and PictureBox, Inc.
photography by Michael Schmelling

Still, how I nearly felt. In the midst of all that looking.

—David Markson, *Wittgenstein's Mistress*

Contents

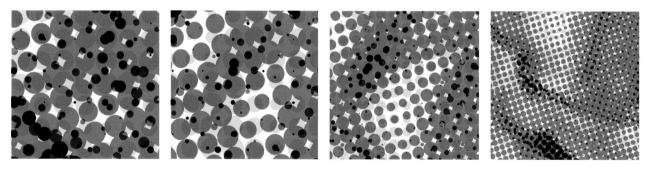

Past the orange roof and turquoise tower, past the immense sunburst of the green and yellow sign, past the golden arches, beyond the low buff building, beside the discreet hut, the dark top hat on the studio window shade, beneath the red and white longitudes of the enormous bucket, coming up to the thick shaft of the yellow arrow piercing the royal-blue field, he feels he is home. Is it Nashville? Elmira, New York? St. Louis County? A Florida key? The Illinois arrowhead? Indiana like a holster, Ohio like a badge? Is he North? St. Paul, Minn.? Northeast? Boston, Mass.? The other side of America? Salt Lake? Los Angeles? At the bottom of the country? The Texas udder? Where? In Colorado's frame? Wyoming like a postage stamp? Michigan like a mitten? The chipped, eroding bays of the Northwest? Seattle? Bellingham, Washington?

Somewhere in the packed masonry of states.

—Stanley Elkin, *The Franchiser*

Interlude, Henry Miller and Fred Tomaselli

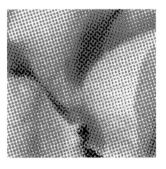 

(Preceding pages) The power supply to the band's
spacious Chicago office/practice space/hideout

The Loft

For me, the loft means space—it gives me space to create, and space for us together as a band to grow an environment that caters to creativity—just a warm place that welcomes exploration. There've been different times with different dynamics in the band when it's ceased to be that, but I think those have been the times it's been really imperative that something changes. When people start to not want to go there, because of a personality, or because of the clutter, or because of whatever, then it's totally useless, it's a waste of money. Now, we have Jason and Matt doing such an amazing job of maintaining it. Jason puts an enormous amount of love into it, making it warm and comfortable, and not accepting that it's finished, ever. It's great. You can go there and within two seconds you can be making sounds on any instrument. The goal, over time, is to get it to where it's more and more immediate, and there's less downtime. And the concept of the studio will eventually be to be able to hit *record* at any time—whatever's happening in the room—and leave a certain amount of stuff miked up all the time, so we can just go, *all right, wow, let's document that*. That, to me, is an ideal way to work. It's very unnatural and requires a lot of method acting to go into a recording studio. It's still real, but there's always that artificiality of it. I wish we owned the whole building and all lived there, like the Monkees. And had a fire pole from floor to floor. It's not going to happen, though. [JT]

That almost extinct relic from a better time: the rec room. And having a place to jam can only help. [JS]

(These and following pages) Photographs on left by Schmelling; pictures on right from the archives of PictureBox and Wilco

Here's a go at my drumming philosophy: I view my drum set not as a defined instrument, but rather a collection of selected sounds that vary according to the musical needs at hand. I think that drums—percussion—can be used not only as a rhythm instrument, but also for color and texture (as in an orchestra). I think that the drum kit hasn't been explored enough outside of the parameters of groove-based jazz or rock and that it has an exciting future. In a rock band, I think as much technique should be amassed as possible and then forgotten, only rearing its head for reasons of musicality or lyrical support. I also like to view the drummer's limbs as a quartet, with each appendage having its own role and responsibility with varying degrees of freedom and dependence. [GK]

Strips of
bamboo
with a
gourd
as a
sound-
box
make

INTENSITY

If you can find the balance between instinct and "thinking," your shit gets rocking. I call this (attempted) balance "Brute Ignorance." It's finding that unique personal sound, chord voicing, or phrasing with a reckless irreverence. When I'm presented with a song that I'm supposed to play keyboards on, my approach is never the same. Frequently I try and play along the first time, which sometimes yields fruit, but I wind up hearing all the mistakes I'm making, and then I stop playing and start listening. Other times, I'll simply listen through the whole song, and then start spouting ideas. [MJ]

Ever since I was little, I thought about music in a very weird, detached kind of way and, at the same time, was hypersensitive to the point where it was hard, painfully hard, to listen to some music because it hurt so much, meant so much to me.

But one of the things I always had thought when I heard great music was, *Okay, if somebody came from outer space and I had to explain what it was like to be human, this is what I would play for them, and say this is what we sound like.* And I think about that when I listen to Alabama Sacred Heart Singers. Stuff like that is really easy to listen to because there's no words, it's just sound. There's also great pieces of rock music. *This is as good as we are.*

Even the Stooges, even the nihilistic stuff. I have my problems with his writing, but Greil Marcus wrote what I think was a great insight into punk rock: "A thousand noes would add up to a giant yes." That made a lot of sense to me—why was it so liberating to listen to, so life affirming? [JT]

PINNA

HAMMOND

olux
Reverb-Amp
MUSICAL INSTRUMENTS

HAVE GUN
WILL
TRAVEL

PREMIUM
PREMIUM
PREMIUM

You

OVAL WINDOW

GRAND CENTRAL TERMINAL
NEW YORK CITY

ZENITH

Bass playing, for me, is really about feel. I try to have some sort of meeting of soul and cerebrum. I don't want to simplify things—some people say, "If you're thinking, you're stinking," but I don't believe that. I try to go with my instinct. It can be McCartney, or it can be as simple as Nashville bass. Basically, I hold down the bottom end, phrase things in an interesting way, and provide harmony, and generally think in terms of the guitars and provide a foundation and harmonic input. But my idea of bass playing is what serves the song. I've had different levels of input over the years, but being part of the moment is enough for me—being part of the ensemble. That's really where the framework for lyrics comes from. I've been able to satisfy several ideas over the years, and frankly, it's just really fun to play with the band.

My favorite bassists have been guys I don't know very much about, like "so-and-so who played on this." Two of those guys are Joe Osborne, from Shreveport, Louisiana, who started with Ricky Nelson and played on probably a hundred songs you can sing—and also from Memphis, Tommy Cogbill, who was in the famous American Studios house band in the '60s, who played with Dusty, Elvis, and lots of others. Listen to him on "Soul Deep," by the Box Tops. Nobody swung like that. [JS]

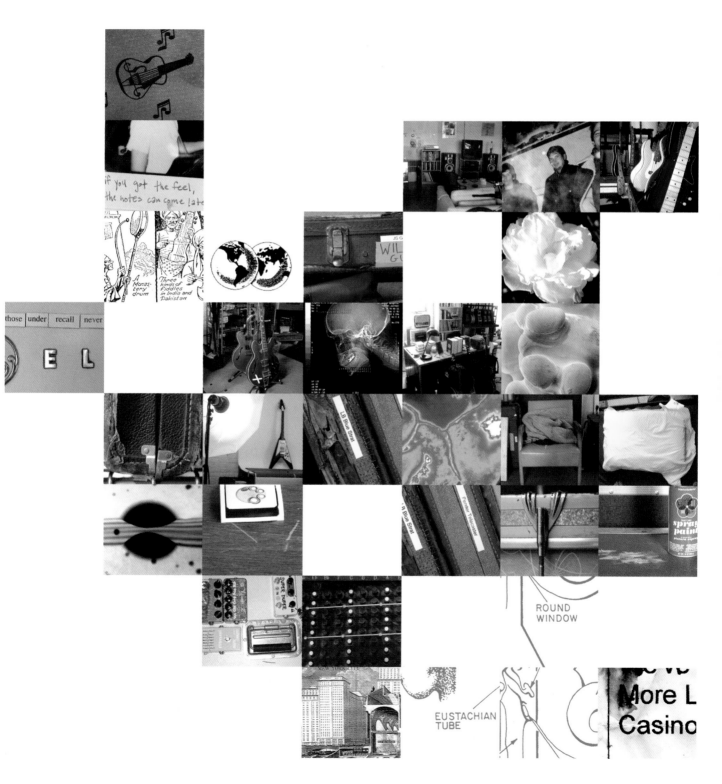

Well air-conditioned and nicely kept, the loft sometimes serves as living quarters for out-of-towners such as ourselves. We slept on couches and cots, watched cable television, and ogled various piles of instruments, books, records, paint-by-numbers, and ephemera. Most of the book discussions occurred between 11:00 PM and 2:00 AM—prime working hours there. It is surprisingly comfy: as much home as office, practice space as workshop. The loft consistently smells oddly fresh and vaguely clean. It is extremely dark and quietly humming at night, and incredibly bright and alive in the morning. While there we: read Flann O'Brien's *The Best of Myles*; listened to Willie Nelson, Judee Sill, T-Rex, Deerhoof, and Genesis (see Appendix II); selected and sequenced The Book CD; listened to stories about ZZ Top and The Band; ate good Thai food and at least one unusually mediocre hot dog; watched the band practice; foolishly turned down the chance to play tambourine with them; made jokes; smoked cigarettes; slept; worried; waited; worked. [PICTUREBOX]

I look at an instrument as a living and breathing organism. Since it is made mostly of wood, it has a life essence to it. It's all feeling and touch. I've been holding them since I was young. I get the most out of taking a guitar that is in ill shape and bringing it back to life. Many guitars have been mistreated but still have a glimmer of hope, and it's important to at least try to make things better. The more a guitar is played, the better it will sound; it needs to get used to being an *instrument* and not a *chair*, so it's difficult when some musicians expect a guitar to play itself. That's why I think most good luthiers would make great shrinks: *it's usually not the guitar*. You need resistance to create tension, and once you discover how much of that a given musician is willing to accept, you can really create a lot of magic for them. It's important for me because I feel my work will outlive me, and I want to leave something of myself that people can respond to—give my organic matter back to balance things out. [FM]

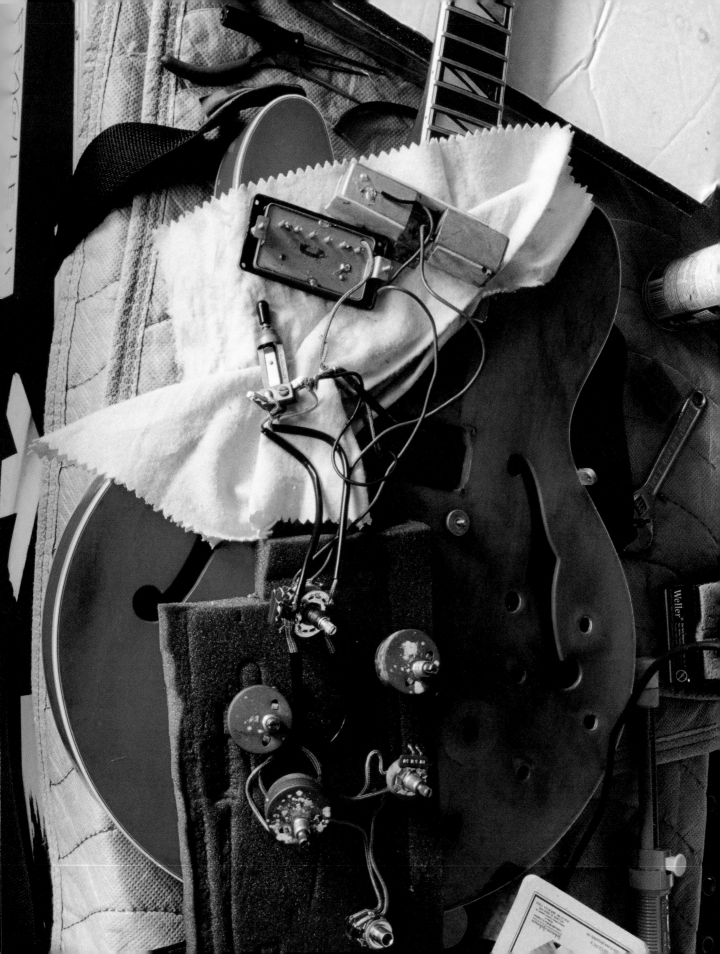

3

The Instruments

I think that there are songs in guitars waiting to come out. You write differently on different types of guitars. The guitars that have stayed closest to me for the longest periods of time have been the ones that just had some kind of intangible aura or feeling about them when I picked them up in the store. I've empowered them, quite a bit, but I also think that they are not just things, in and of themselves. [JT]

1. This is my electronics rack and stick bag. The rack has my sampler, my drum brain, and the effects units that I use on my drums live. I've always loved playing in rock bands. It feels good and keeps me in shape. Playing in a band takes a certain degree of self-confidence because you have to believe that you can actually do this and make a living despite the insecurities and volatility of it all, and you have to believe that people actually want to hear what you're trying to express. It also takes a sense of humility, so your ego doesn't get out of hand and people don't get sick of you. [GK]

2. This is the venerable bass of the group. It was Jeff's Uncle Tupelo bass, and I used it in Uncle Tupelo as well, and then throughout Wilco—"Sunken Treasure," "I Must Be High" (the first song we recorded), right up to "Kicking Television." It's a punk-rock bass. [JS] It was rode hard and put away wet. The head stock of this bass is chewed from years of using it as a drumstick on cymbal edges. It is a Fender Precision from the '60s with a badass bridge that Jeff put on. I was told that when he got it, it had a Van Halen-type paint job on it. That didn't fly, so now it's black. The back of this bass tells most of the story and most of the reason why guitars and belt buckles don't get along. [FM]

3. These are homemade or customized drumsticks and mallets. *(Left to right:)* Bamboo rods (softer than regular rods); super-ball skewers (these make the drums moan); split sticks, with ping-pong balls filled with shotgun shot (soft stick and shaker in one); homemade broom sticks (years before they were commercially available); ball whisks (amazing); and clicker sticks (these are Korean sticks used to strike the body for increased circulation). I use these when we play acoustically in the loft or at radio stations, and at solo shows (see Appendix III). [GK]

4. These are all antique noisemakers from antique-toy stores and junk shops. Miiri, my wife, got me a couple of them, as did Dawson Prater from Locust Records. I like them because they're not typical, overused, cliché percussion instruments. Most people haven't heard these sounds before, so hopefully they add an unexpected fresh atmosphere to the song. I use these live mainly on "Sunken Treasure," "Poor Places," and "Reservations," as well as on solo stuff. [GK]

5. This head led to the prepared drumheads that I make. Three candle trays and an antique rice bowl attached with Velcro to the head. I used this on improvised shows, and a couple of times with Jeff at his solo shows. More sounds with no extra space needed (see Appendix III). [GK]

6. My favorite hubcap. I got this at an all-hubcap store in Libertyville, Illinois, just up the street from the high school where I was teaching at the time. I chose it because of its sound, of course, but also because of all the various textures that it has. It's very versatile. This is the hubcap used in the main drum part in "I Am Trying to Break Your Heart." [GK]

7. An old piano with its guts removed. Once used as a keyboard holder for Leroy. Now it's on hiatus. [MJ]

8. Most of the amplifiers that the band uses are of the tube variety. They are preferable because tubes distort a signal—a guitar signal, let's say—in a nice, perhaps more classic-sounding way. They are based on designs that were perfected a long time ago. The simplicity of tube circuitry allows easy fixing, modification, and restoration. There are all kinds of tubes, the most important being the tubes in a preamplifier, which give you your wicked tone. And then there are the big ones that give you the loudness—the amplification you so desire. This tube tester will tell you a few things, but it won't tell you everything. The best tube tester for guitar amps is a chopstick (like what you get with your sushi) and your ears. Tubes can pick up interference from the outside world and mess with your sound. When that happens, it's called microphonics. It's fairly easy to catch that, though, because when you tap on a microphonic tube, the tapping sound will go through your speakers. Everything else is pretty obvious to the senses,

but not necessarily to this tester: strange sounds, glowing tubes, and any other out-of-the-ordinary stuff. So on this tester, a *good* tube might be *bad*. A *bad* tube goes into the trash, or into your surplus/found-electronics sculptures. And if you have exhausted all possibility of tube failure, then your tube-man sculpture may acquire resistors for hair and capacitors for legs, the further you troubleshoot. [MZ]

9. It's Jeff's head—he's been using it a lot lately. His head is always breaking. You can understand how much of a pain it is to get into someone's head, because when you finally need to, you have to get into the center—where it glows, of course! [MZ]

10. A gift. Like all great gifts, it was something I never could have bought for myself. Paul Westerberg warned that guitars like this can give you VD. [JT] When I started working for Jeff, I thought it would be fun to see him playing it. But at the time he didn't like the way it felt. I gave it a look-see and took off, and when I returned to the loft he was playing it and having a good time. So it came out on the road and was used for a while. We joked about putting *Midlife Crisis* across the front. The crowds really seem to like it when he puts it on. It brings out another side of his playing. [FM]

11. This is the first great guitar I ever owned. Used almost exclusively on *A.M.* [JT] This is an older Gibson J45 that's been stripped of its finish. This one needs some loving before it will be used live or as a recording guitar. But, all the same, it's very close to the heart. The shape of an acoustic guitar is very important in relation to what kind of sound it will produce. Gibson made many of these guitars with this shape, body style, etc., and the shape of this guitar is a real trademark sound for Gibson. Just think of the inside being a mini-auditorium—the shape of the walls and ceiling, as well as the length and depth of the guitar, have a huge effect on its sound. This guitar is classified as a dreadnought, a name taken from the old days of large wooden boats and battleships. [FM]

12. This is one of the first basses I had in Wilco—the Firebird, with one pickup. I just dated it as 1965. I love that thing. I got it at Wayne's (Midwest Buy & Sell), where we've gotten most of our stuff. This bass was on lots of *Being There*, and at least two songs on every record. "A Shot in the Arm." It has a hoofey sound. [JS]

13. Different-colored picks are the only way to keep track of the days of the week on the road. (White ones on Sunday, and tortoise-shell on Saturday.) [JT]

14. This is one of three cases. When we are touring, I take as much as I can. You never know what to expect at any time. If it wasn't with us, we would need it. Guitar repair and upkeep require many things, and luckily, many of them are small. It's very specialized and many of the tools are similar to what a jeweler might have. Guitars are functional jewelry. The essentials are many things you would expect—such as screwdrivers, rules, hammers, soldering irons, etc. The other stuff is top secret! [FM]

15. My other favorite early guitar. Used at least once on every Wilco album to date. [JT] This is a '50s Gibson J45, known in the Wilco camp as #2. It used to be #1, but the sound of an acoustic instrument is known to change over time, and not always for the better. Not to say it has a bad sound—Jeff used to play this guitar live quite often, but then gravitated toward his other J45. Note the photos of his family on the bass side of the fingerboard. It has been used as a writing tool for many years. [FM]

16. The Telefunken Gavotte. I bought it for Jeff as a birthday present a few years back. At the time, I was very into collecting old German tube radios—Grundigs and Telefunkens, mostly. I still have quite a few, and have given several as gifts. Anyway, this one sits, to this day, in the Wilco loft behind Jeff's desk. I absolutely love the way it looks—and frankly, it sounds even better. [TM] Mostly tuned between stations. [JT]

1.

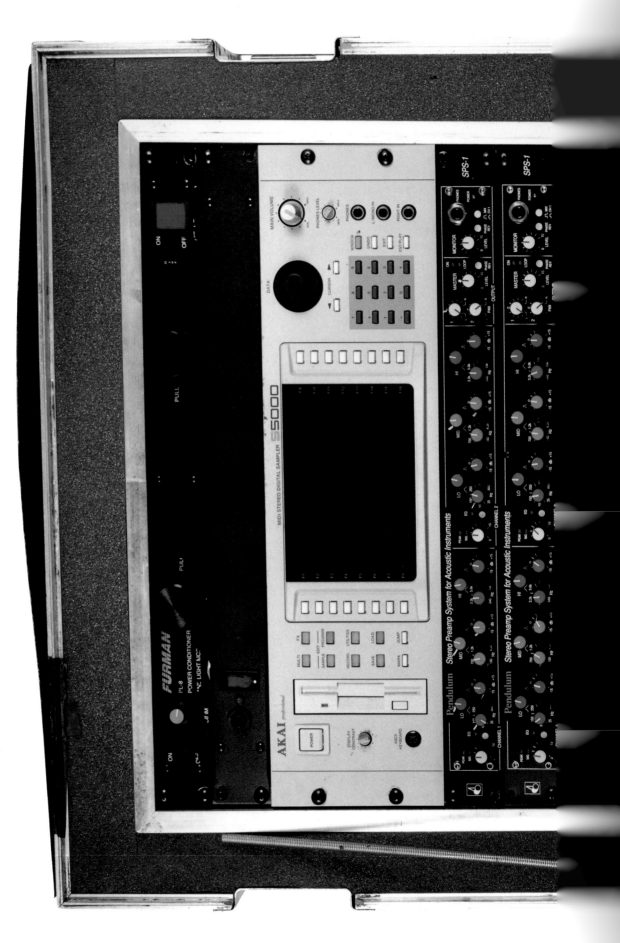

2.

3.

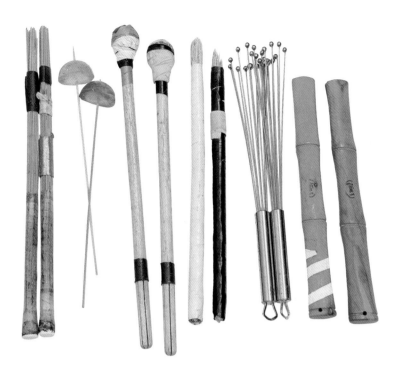

4.

7.

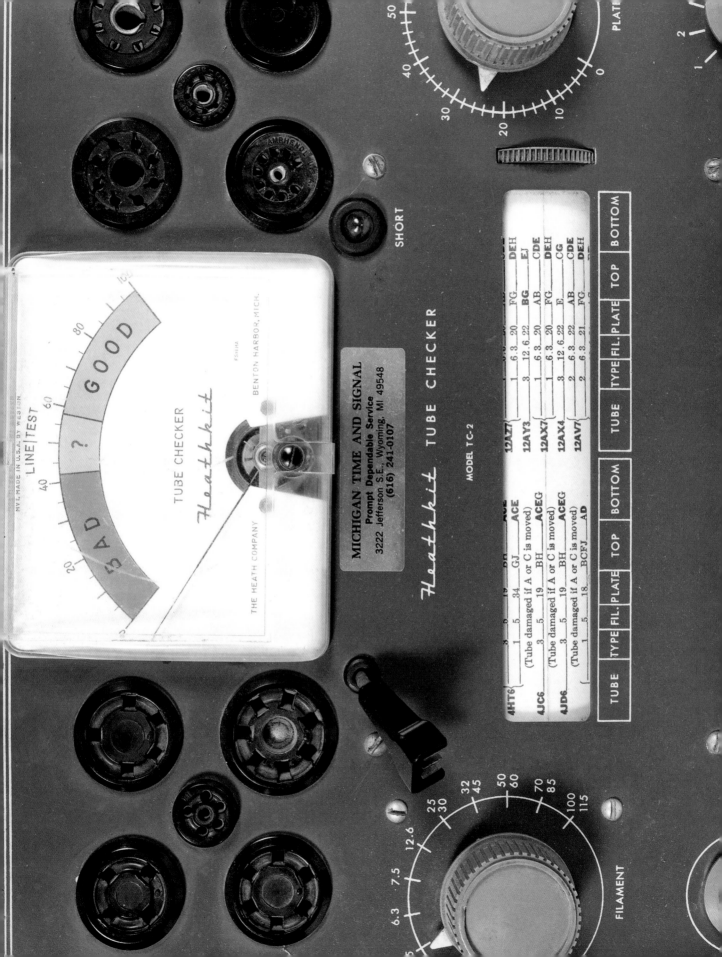

10.

11.

12.

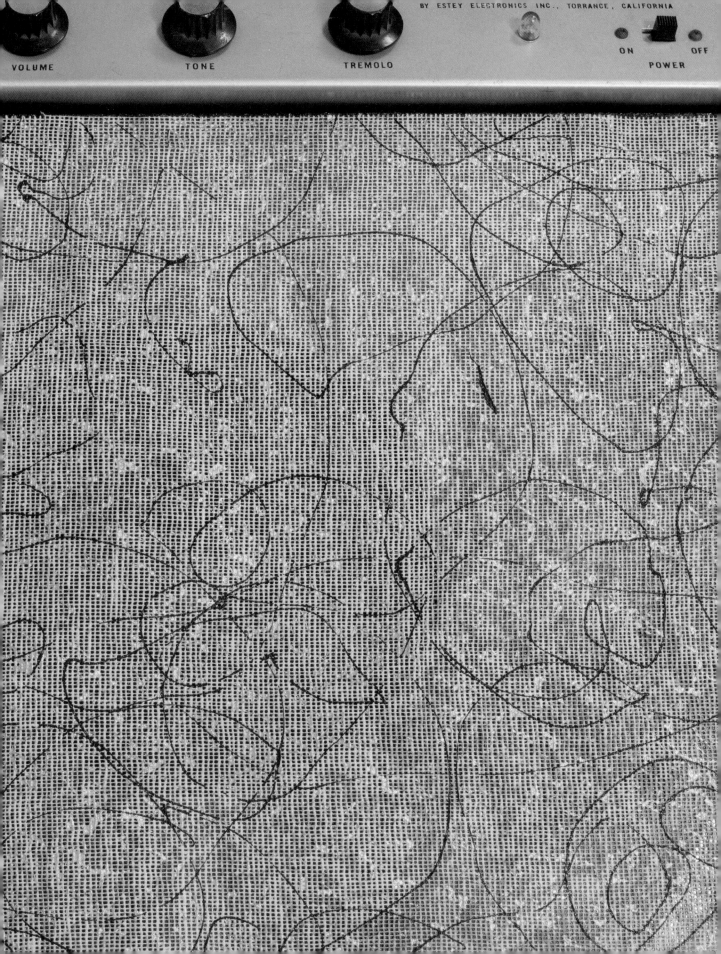

VOLUME   TONE   TREMOLO   BY ESTEY ELECTRONICS INC., TORRANCE, CALIFORNIA

ON   POWER   OFF

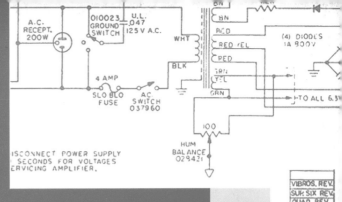

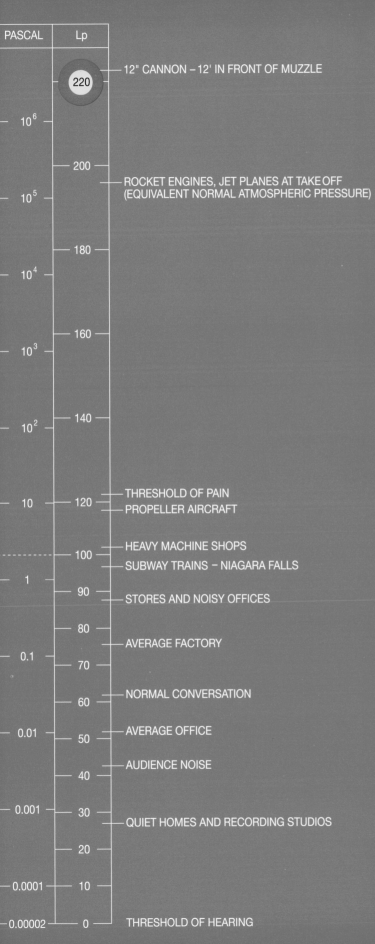

PASCAL	Lp	
	220	12" CANNON – 12' IN FRONT OF MUZZLE
10^6		
	200	
10^5		ROCKET ENGINES, JET PLANES AT TAKEOFF (EQUIVALENT NORMAL ATMOSPHERIC PRESSURE)
	180	
10^4		
	160	
10^3		
	140	
10^2		
	120	THRESHOLD OF PAIN
10		PROPELLER AIRCRAFT
	100	HEAVY MACHINE SHOPS
1		SUBWAY TRAINS – NIAGARA FALLS
	90	STORES AND NOISY OFFICES
	80	
0.1		AVERAGE FACTORY
	70	
	60	NORMAL CONVERSATION
0.01		
	50	AVERAGE OFFICE
	40	AUDIENCE NOISE
0.001		
	30	QUIET HOMES AND RECORDING STUDIOS
	20	
0.0001		
	10	
0.00002	0	THRESHOLD OF HEARING

The Sound:
A talk with Stan Doty and Jason Tobias about live sound.

4

WHAT THEY DO

[SD] I'm a house-sound guy. I mix bands out front, I place mikes in their spots. Basically, I'm there to help every audience member have a good experience.

Wilco is a complicated band to mix. Jeff plays old-school at times, and other times he's totally cutting-edge. It's tricky but refreshing: it's great to see bands that don't get stagnant. What exactly he wants to say with the sound, I'm not sure. That's probably very deep.

[JaT] I have a lot of responsibility. I'm the production manager, drum tech, and monitor guy. My routine generally starts when I wake up. I have to find out where to park the bus, where to load in, who my contact person is. I have to squash any bad feelings from people with bad attitudes who are working at the venue just because they got called in. Then we spend four hours loading in and setting up. We set up the PA, set all the gear up, bring out all the monitors,

Eardrum illustrations by Eve Madsen, from *An Aural Atlas*, 1946

(Preceding pages, right) Magnatone amplifier
(This and following pages) Schematics for a Fender amplifier

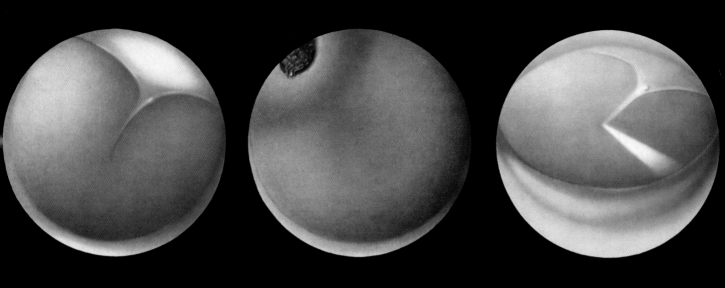

and then Stan tunes up the front of the house so that at the four-hour mark, the band can just come out and play.

Every day we also do a line check, which entails going through all the instruments, and making sure that each one has a clean signal. If somebody plays guitar, we have to make sure he's getting everything in that signal smoothly—that it's not going *crackle* unless it's supposed to.

[SD] With some of the computer stuff, I'm not sure if it's supposed to *crackle* or not. For a while there, when the band was working out their new, more computer-based sounds, we were hearing stuff that—well, you cross your arms, and you wait.

[JAT] When we check everything, it's always good to start from an assessment of the sound and equipment of the night before so we can address any ongoing problems. After all, if the band walks in and everything is all over the place, it takes away from the time they should be jamming or rehearsing. And we shouldn't have to stop rehearsals either. A lot of times they're working on new material, so if you have to stop, you've stymied their growth.

Our job should be transparent: they shouldn't know that we're there. The music should just happen. So, after all of the technical checks, we move into the sound check and then the sound-practice rehearsal.

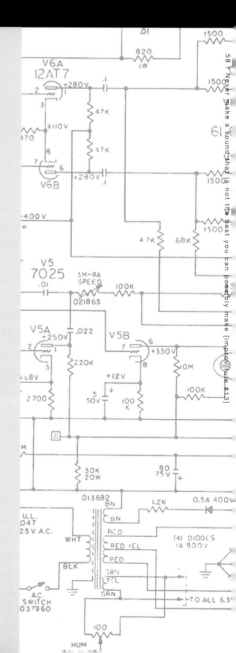

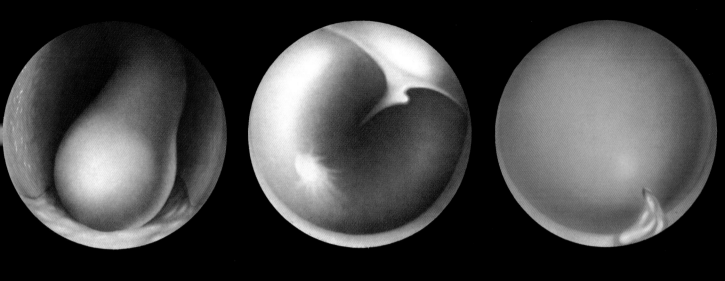

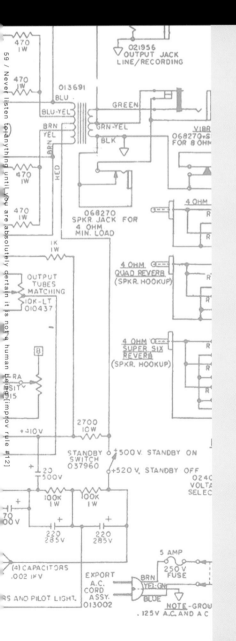

[SD] Sound checks are usually one or two songs. Then we do sound practices, which are rehearsals, maybe changing up some of the songs, or going over songs from the night before that the band struggled with or didn't really feel. They'll do that for two hours. Generally, by the end, everybody's happy. Then we break for an hour or so and have dinner. Then the doors open, and I walk around and basically make sure that everybody's doing what they're supposed to be to get the opening act out on time. After the opening act, it goes over to changeover, then Wilco, then after the show you tear it down, load it out, and drive on to the next city. It's like a routine—except on days off, when we get really drunk.

WHY THEY DO IT

[JAT] What I love to do the most is sound. And with this job, I have to compartmentalize a little bit because there are so many other things that need to get done. And I try to still mix the sound at clubs in Chicago when we're not on the road. When we were doing the album, I mixed maybe four times in three months—that was the longest I've ever gone without "practicing." The first couple shows back are always a little rough.

I do it for the thrill of just being a part of it, because you're not really facilitating that much. There are things—sometimes difficult things—that you just need to do in order for it to happen. But that's our job.

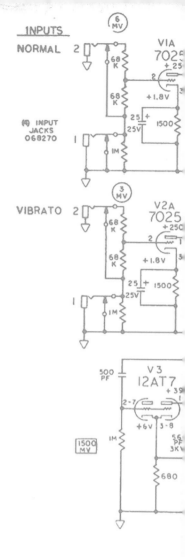

[SD] I love it because you're in control of everybody's ambience for the evening. I love to see people bopping. If heads are moving, if people are enjoying it, then that's really what it's all about. Each room's a little different, and if you can achieve your same sound in each room, or come close, or at least get to the point where that room sounds as good as it ever has, then you've been successful.

THE SHOW

[JaT] During the show, Matt and Frankie are taking care of guitars, changes, and tunings and things. I'm onstage doing monitors, which are the speakers that enable the band to hear each other while they perform. The guys have eight or ten mixes that they need to hear. Stan mixes to the people; I have to mix to each individual band member. So I'm basically mixing what everybody needs to hear, but trying to keep it consistent with everybody else in the band.

[SD] It all starts with the band. If there's a good mix going onstage, the band doesn't have to worry about it. And then it translates better to the audience—or at least has a chance to. One of the greatest things about this band is that they go from low-fi to high-fi, low dynamics to high dynamics, cutting-edge stuff to old-school.

It's wonderful to mix out front. "Passenger Side" or "Casino Queen"—they're just great, old-school songs. On those I do a straightforward mix. If a guy comes in for a lead and it's not loud enough, you just pump it up. There are certain set rules. Same thing goes for the new-school stuff, too. They've got some wonderful stereo signals and stuff like that—accents in the songs.

The main thing is that it's the band's mix, it's not the sound guy's mix. A lot of sound guys forget that. You translate, and hopefully you're translating what the band wants. That right there will judge how long you stay with the band. The main thing is attitude.

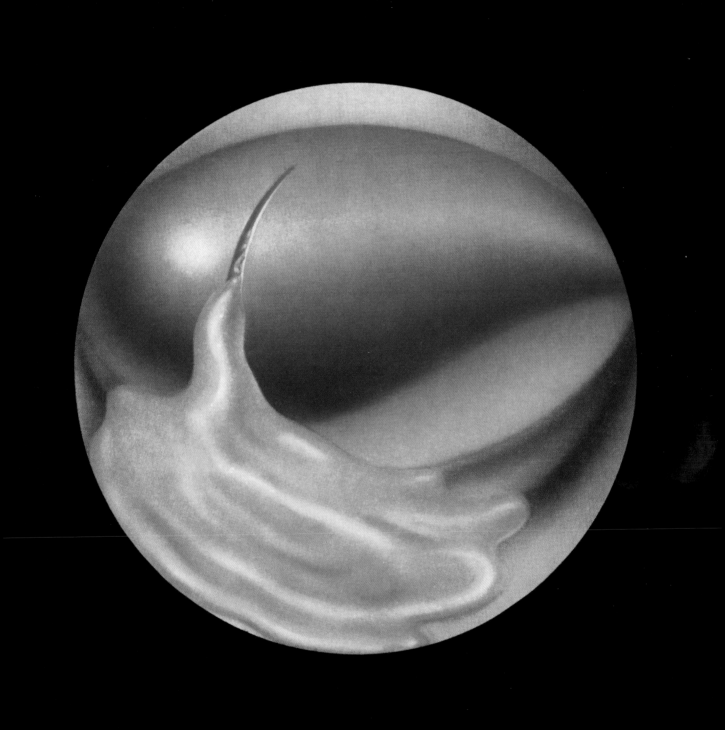

The Angel Is
My Watermark

by Henry Miller

Images by Fred Tomaselli

P EOPLE OFTEN ASK: "IF YOU HAD YOUR LIFE TO LIVE all over again, would you do this or that?" Meaning—would you repeat the same mistakes? As for *les amours* I am not so sure. But as to water colors, yes. Because the important thing which I learned, through making water colors, was not to worry, not to care too much. We don't have to turn out a masterpiece every day. To paint is the thing, not to make masterpieces. Even the Creator, when he made his perfect universe, had to learn not to care too much. Certainly when he created Man he gave himself a prolonged headache.

And Man, when he attains fulfillment, or a state of grace, if you like, ceases to play the Creator. I mean that he no longer feels compelled to draw, paint, describe in words or music what he sees around him. He can let things be. He discovers, just by looking the world in the face, that everything is a bit of a masterpiece. Why paint? For whom? Enjoy what you see. That's quite enough. The man who can do this is an accomplished artist. The rest of us, we who must sign our names to everything we touch, are simply apprentices. Sorcerers' apprentices. For though we pretend to be instructing others how to see, hear, taste and feel, what we are really doing most of the time is to feed the ego. We refuse to remain anonymous, like the men who made the cathedrals. No, we want to see our names spelled out in neon lights. And we never refuse money for our efforts. Even when we have nothing more to say, we go on writing, painting, singing, dancing, always angling for the spotlight.

And now here I come with my water colors—and my name in big letters. Another sinner. Another ego. I must confess it gives me great pleasure. I shan't be a hypocrite and say, "I hope it gives you pleasure also." *Pour moi, c'est un fait accompli, c'est tout.* I waited twenty years to see these water colors gathered together in a book. Frankly, I had hoped there might be fifty or a hundred reproduced instead of a dozen or so. However, better half a loaf than none, as the saying goes.

The best part of it all is that I am not obliged to wait until I die. I can view them now, *ici-bas*, with the eyes of a sinner, a wastrel, a profligate, rather than with the eyes of an angel or a ghost. That's something. Looking at them from another perspective, perhaps they will teach me something about true humility.

Of one thing I am certain…now that my dream has been realized I will enjoy whatever I do more than ever before. I have no ambition to become a masterful painter. I simply want to go on painting, more and more, even though I may be committing a crime against the Holy Ghost. The nearer I get to the grave the more time I have to waste. Nothing is important now, in the sense it once was. I can lean to the right or left without danger of capsizing. I can go off the course, too, if I wish, because my destination is no longer a fixed one. As those two delightful bums in *Waiting for Godot* say time and again:

"*On y va?*"

"*Oui.*"

And no one budges.

I realize, of course, that these vagabond reflections and observations are hardly in the Teutonic tradition. They are not even American, if I know my people. But doesn't it make you feel good to read them? And, suppose it's all cockeyed, what I say. What difference? At least you know where I stand. And *you*, are you standing on solid ground? Prove it!

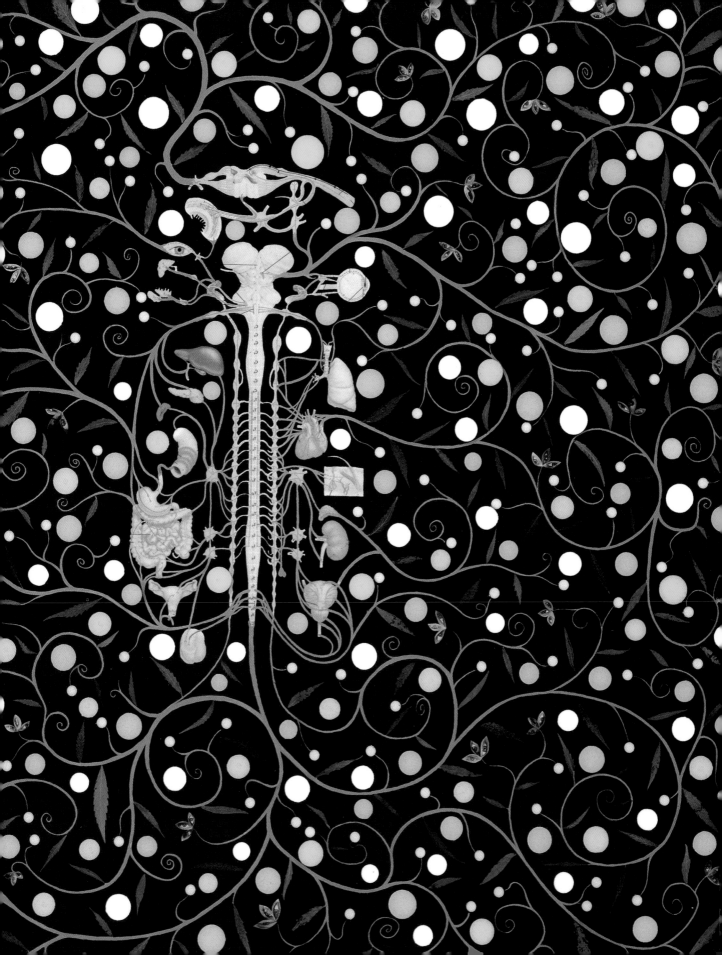

Long ago, when I was making merry writing *Black Spring*, I was already reveling in the fact that the world about me was going to pieces. From the time that I was old enough to think, I had a hunch that this was so. Then I came upon Oswald Spengler. He confirmed my inner convictions. (And what a really good time I had reading him, reading about the "decline of the west." It was better, honestly, than reading the Bhagavad-Gita. It bucked me up.) Nor did I have the cheek then to say as Rimbaud: *"Moi, je suis intact!"* It didn't matter to me whether I was intact or falling to pieces. I was attending a spectacle: the crumbling of our civilization. Today the disintegration is proceeding even more rapidly, thanks to our technic and efficiency. Today everybody is writing about it, even our school children. But they don't get much fun out of it, have you noticed?

What I recommend for the few remaining years that are left us is—to piss the time away enjoyably. Make water colors, for example. No need to sign your name to them, if you don't wish to. Just turn them out one after the other, good, bad, indifferent, no matter. Nero fiddled while Rome burned. Making water colors is much better. You don't harm anybody, you don't make a spectacle of yourself, you don't collaborate with the enemy. When you go to bed you will sleep soundly, not toss all night long. You may find your appetite improved too. You may even find yourself sinning with greater zest—enjoying it, I mean.

What I am trying to say in my offhand way is that in fair weather or foul the men who make the least fuss do more to save what is worth saving—and how much is worth saving, do you ever stop to think?—than those who push us about because they think they have the answer to everything. When you put your mind to such a simple, innocent thing, for example, as making a water color, you lose some of the anguish which derives from being a member of a world gone mad. Whether you paint flowers, stars, horses or angels you acquire respect and admiration for all the elements which go to make up our universe. You don't call flowers friends and stars enemies, or horses Communists and angels Fascists. You accept them for what they are and you praise God that they are what they are. You desist from improving the world or even yourself. You learn to see not what you want to see but what is. And what is is usually a thousand times better than what might be or ought to be. If we could stop tampering with the universe we might find it a far better world than we think it to be. After all, we've only occupied it a few hundred million years, which is to say that we are just beginning to get acquainted with it. And if we continue another billion years there is nothing to assure us that we will eventually know it. In the beginning as in the end it remains a mystery. And the mystery exists or thrives in every smallest part of the universe. It has nothing to do with size or distance, with grandeur or remoteness. Everything hinges upon how you look at things.

The question which emerges with every work of art that is turned out is: "Is there more to what we see than meets the eye?" And the answer is always yes. In the humblest object we can find what we seek—beauty, truth, reality, divinity. The artist does not create these attributes, he discovers them in the process of painting. When he realizes this he can go on painting without danger of sinning, because he then also knows that to paint or not to paint is the same thing. One doesn't sing because he hopes one day to appear in an opera; one sings because one's lungs are full of joy. It's wonderful to listen to a great performance, but it's even more wonderful to encounter in the street a happy vagabond who can't stop singing because his heart is full of joy. Nor does your happy vagabond expect any monetary reward for his efforts. He doesn't know the meaning of effort. No one can be paid to give of his joy, it's always freely given.

Live: Auditorium Theater, Chicago

Having toured behind *Yankee Hotel Foxtrot* for two years, Wilco ended that journey with two hometown concerts at Auditorium Theater on September 19 and 20, 2003.

I'm convinced that very, very few people in the world know the rock and roll I'm singing about. I'm singing about what *I* think of as rock and roll, so there's probably only one person who knows what that is, and that's me. But rock and roll is such a loaded term—it's like singing about God, about something that has come to mean something very powerful and spiritual in a lot of people's lives. But it's narrower in its scope to some people, and it's a cliché to some people. It's something almost too ambiguous to do. You shouldn't put it in a poem or a song. If you want to get rid of ambiguities, rock and roll would be one of the first things you'd have to get rid of. I keep putting it in because it's such a huge part of my formative years. I'm so defined by it…troubled by it. I don't know if I am troubled by it *anymore*. I was troubled by it at one time very much—I thought it was debilitating, being defined by rock and roll. I really thought it was no more noble to be defined by it than to be defined by a lot of fashion or something. I've been concerned with choosing one's terms of identity and self-definition. People who look a certain way have their identity formed around something that isn't exactly an accurate image of themselves. I want to cut through all of that bullshit.

I was turned on to rock and roll at an early age, like many, many millions of people, but turned on in such an aggressive way that, over time, it felt like a burden. I think there are two ways out of it. The path that most people take is to become a doctor and forget about it all. Or some people reduce things, make distinctions and categories, and say, "That's not rock and roll." They find what's narrow and manageable. The more liberating and accurate way is expansive, to start trying to include more and more in your definition. Rock and roll would not be *rock and roll* anymore. It is what it really is—music. And it's the impulse to make music, which is eternal. When you look at it that way, and think, *okay, I can appreciate Slayer as being a part of this continuum, Django Reinhardt*—they all express themselves with noise, or with sound. It's crazy how hard that is to stick to, to remind yourself of, because we're so geared toward judgment—and we have to judge and make distinctions so as to not go insane, swim around in this sea, this unbelievable, infinite pot of information. One of the reasons it's hard to maintain that kind of expansiveness about it is because so much of rock and roll is contextual—and context is a really hard thing to subvert.

Art doesn't exist in discreet moments in time. Its context is more expansive than that. The world will make something out of it over a day, or a hundred years. What we think of something now could change in ten years. Look at a band like Abba, who were considered the worst thing in the world. Take it out of that context and just look at it as human beings making sounds, and it's like, *why the fuck? This is so unbelievably joyous and great and as good as anything ever.* I'm just pontificating.… I feel like Alan Alda in *Crimes and Misdemeanors*—"Comedy is tragedy plus time." [JT]

Handwriting here and elsewhere taken from the daybooks of Tony Margherita

With audiences, I think you just hope for the best. I don't really know anything more than that. Sometimes people like it, and sometimes they don't. If something you've created makes you feel something, you have to have faith that it has that potential for other people. The only extent that I will think about the audience—well, I'd be lying if I said that there aren't many, many inhibiting processes of thought that relate to being conscious of an audience—but the only one that I think is valid and informative and one that is healthy or that contributes in any way is the gentle reminding thought that *you are a listener as well*. I am my own audience, and I want to move myself. When you make stuff, the idea of it being a conversation is the most accurate analogy you can have to make music that you put out into the world. You can't think about it being the world. You think about it being one consciousness. Your voice or your song enters only one consciousness at a time. Boil it down to that one person, and just try and tell them the truth. Try and tell them as straight as you can what you're thinking about, and how you feel. The service that is provided for me by other people's music has been

that I can identify my feelings, and that makes you more human—to have someone articulate things for you. Or even just give you a place to be true, which is in your imagination.

It's weird to talk about, because I think this is a lot more cerebral than a lot of people are comfortable with when imagining what goes into the writing of a piece of music. We're talking about intentions, and I've obviously thought about it a lot. I have intentions. I have artistic intent that I want to be evident in my music. It's a very different thing than something that truly transcends whatever it was initially. One of the reasons that something like Elvis can truly transcend time and audiences is that most people who investigate it don't think he had any intentions, so they can reject everything, and it's a clean slate. And, by the same token, people who aren't really thinking about it don't have to. That's the appeal. They put the needle down on those records and a universe is revealed—a way to see things that's just a visceral force of nature. I guess they call that the real deal. [JT]

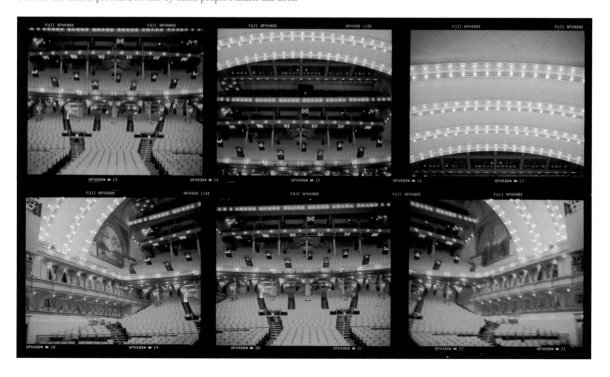

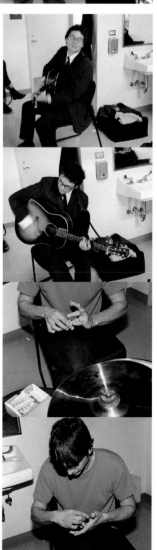

I love playing like this. It's a warmup, but also really informative because we can all hear each other so well. You can really focus on the lyrics. Also, it forces me to be creative, because my setup is so limited. We have dreamed of touring like this on many occasions. It'll happen someday. This is the only way that Jeff and I played when I first met him—when Loose Fur started. We've tried this approach in the studio, too, on occasion. I love this drum setup. This is the exact type of drum kit that I used for years of touring and recording with Birddog and Edith Frost. It's very similar to my solo setup, too. [GK]

The backstage jams can be more stressful than the actual show, oddly enough. More often than not, we'll be going over a song that I'm not a hundred percent on, and I'll be making mistakes, jotting down notes and balancing the keyboard on my lap, thinking, *shit, I have to go do this for a theater full of humans in twenty minutes!* But once the show starts, all that anxiety just falls away, like the papery skin of a garlic clove once you've smashed it. [MJ]

Everything sounds best before we hit the stage. [JT]

I tape up because I play much harder on tour than I do when we're just playing at home or when I play solo. I guess I'm a wimp. I get really bad blisters sometimes and have to tape up so they don't affect my playing. I usually get a few small injuries on every tour—just bloody hands from accidentally hitting a drum rim or cymbal or something. I honestly never know when that happens until I see the blood all over my drumheads. It's not usually that painful—it looks worse than it is because I'm not paying attention to stop the bleeding. I think it probably bums out Jason, though, since he's got to tune and change the heads. I'm very lucky that I haven't had any muscle injuries so far—that's why warming up is so important to me. [GK]

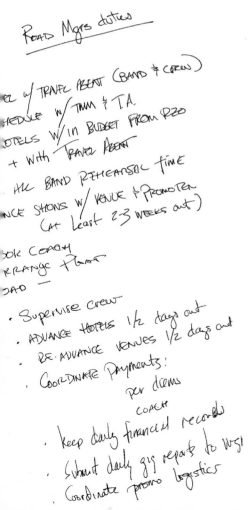

Road Mgrs duties

EL w/ TRAVEL AGENT (BAND + CREW)
HEDULE w/ TMM + T.A.
OTELS w/ IN BUDGET FROM RZO
+ WITH TRAVEL AGENT
ALL BAND REHEARSAL TIME
NCE SHOWS w/ VENUE + PROMOTER
(AT LEAST 2-3 WEEKS OUT)

OK COACH
RRANGE PLANE
JAD —

• Supervise crew
• ADVANCE HOTELS 1/2 days out
• RE-ADVANCE VENUES 1/2 days out
• Coordinate Payments:
        per diems
            COACH
• keep daily financial records
• Submit daily gig reports to WJ!
• Coordinate promo logistics

I've been across the country about twenty times. Is it true that only ten percent of Americans have passports? I love the sights here, but I don't have a problem leaving for a while, if you know what I mean. I haven't seen the Grand Canyon or done the Four Corners drive. I do remember seeing something new the last drive out, where the West starts, about forty miles west of Amarillo. It's just Texas, and then, all of a sudden, you come to a rise—and on the other side, it looks like the West. I guess all the waiting around is normal for me. You have to get out and about, or go insane. David Byrne is an avid bicyclist; he goes out immediately after arrival and spends all day on the bike, then arrives for check. It's that window in the morning between arrival and sound check when you have time to see the town you're in, which is a huge plus about touring, for me—even in Orlando.

It's funny—this life of music has sort of unfolded for me. I was always interested in music, but I had a defeatist idea about it. Some of my favorite bands were just abject failures. The opposite has happened to me; it's been a long career, a solid career. I always thought

there'd be another career, that I'd get rock and roll out of my system and go back to grad school for English or something, but I realized recently that I'm probably too old to go to back now. In 2000 or so I realized that music was probably what I would do forever. It's that realization you have: "This is what I do." It's a life in music, and it's a strange joke that's been played on me—that I'm thankful for. [JS]

Once we're in the venue, the waiting can be kind of boring. My mind is on the show, so I can't really do anything productive. But it's a bit different now. We usually have a mini-setup backstage. I like that much more. We get to play and run through stuff or work on new songs. As long as we're all away from home it makes sense to play as much as we possibly can—be productive. When we don't have instruments backstage, I'll still play on a practice pad for a chunk of time to warm up and get my hands in shape. It helps, too. I can play much better at the end of a tour after all that practice time. Even though all the waiting is a drag, by the time I get out on stage I'm really ready to play and hit some stuff. [GK]

Thax, a Chicago poet. We have a road case for him. [JT]

Cary Grant   oc Vinyl
         953 3704

1 Jeff P   6 Justin Burr 2278429
2 Bob A.   7 Puchumm
3 JL 2604700   8 Bob Hodus   call fi hmm
4 F Riley   901 526 c
5 Chingo   9 Nuw W. 2488709   x1112
  E. Grymm
             10 Joanna D Azzus
             [BP list]   956 2105

Wardrobe probably only matters to us. The last time I dressed up, it was a red sharkskin suit on the Jools Holland show for the BBC, and as I came down the stairs to the commissary, I saw Van Morrison, also on the show, sitting square in front of me. I nodded and smiled, and he shook his head, *no*. I never wore that suit again. [JS]

I like ties for weddings and the occasional "night out." As a Sinatra fan, there's certainly a part of me that would love to sport the black tie every night. However, suits plus rock bands equals dangerous territory. I'm still searching for the right blend of fancy and broken. [MJ]

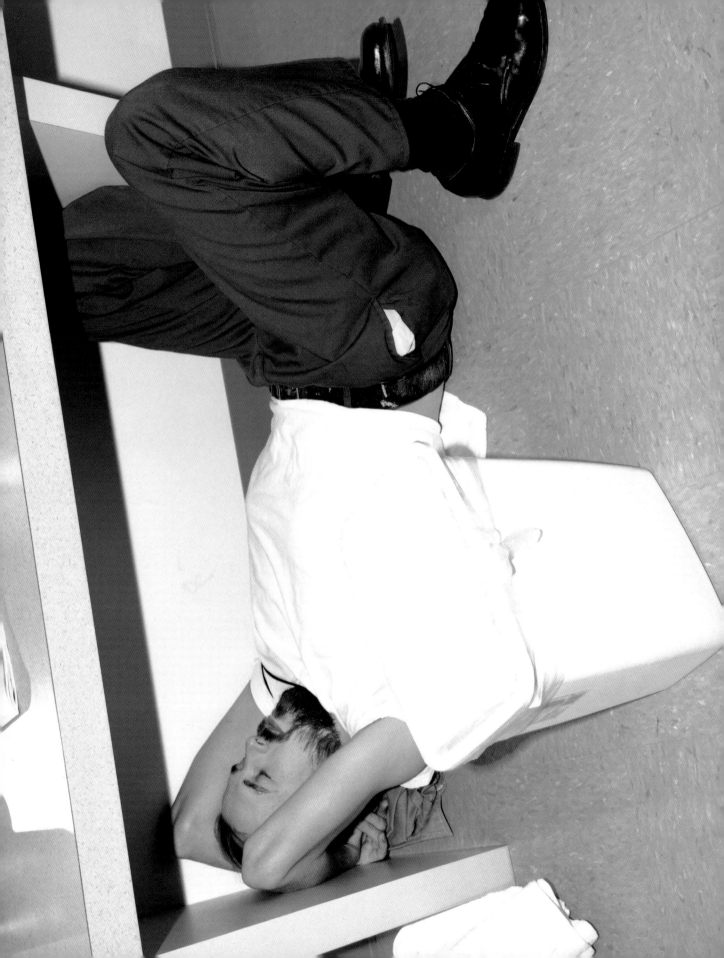

(Preceding page) The faster I can write a set list, the better the show will be, usually. We used to settle on a set and play it—with minor changes—for an entire tour. Now we feel more comfortable being uncomfortable—and try really hard to have enough material at the ready to change things up significantly from night to night. We still get lazy, though. [JT]

I fail almost every time that I try to make a set list, because I just think of what I would want to hear if I were in the audience, instead of considering who plays what guitar and what key the song is in, etc.— the logistics. That stuff is important, but it's just too difficult to keep track of all of it. I'm usually too occupied with my gear to notice all the different guitars rotating in and out of the set. I always try to get the guys to play the recorded sequence. For example, if there's time for a longer encore, I'll suggest *Being There*, side one, or the first three or four from *A.M.* I realize that that approach is not very creative, but I can't help it. I'm also a fan of varying the set as much as possible from night to night. However, when we find a combination of a few songs that go really well together, we tend to keep it intact for a few shows.

"Misunderstood" is my favorite song to play live because I get to hit as hard as I possibly can. That was my favorite Wilco song before joining. Also: "I Am Trying to Break Your Heart," because I get to play an interlocking drum/vibes part; "Poor Places"—I switch sticks and percussion instruments with each section, and just because I love it; "Radio Cure" and "Pot Kettle Black," because my parts are really challenging. [GK]

Playing live allows for the experience of that personal "speaking to me" lyrical content on a big scale. It's like a private conversation with a lot of the world. It's wonderful. I had that same reaction when I first heard Uncle Tupelo. I was touched personally. It wasn't as direct as Wilco, but a lot of my favorite writers are like that. They might not be as overt as Jeff, but a lot of people are looking for that and want to have conversations like that. It's always the freshest stuff that I like to play the most. We've been around so long—I feel like Foghat or something. But, of the older stuff, I do like to play "Far Far Away" and "She's a Jar."

There are moments when you forget you are playing in front of people, completely—whether from having some sort of connective moment with the rest of the band, or with one or two other people in the band, to having some sort of insulated, pneumatic moment, where it could feel as private as the bedroom of your apartment. [JS]

(Overleaf, left) These three things control time. Mix will give you a mixture of dryness to delayed sound. Time of delay can be varied, from short to long. Feedback is the length of the time delay after the fact, until complete decay. This is one of my resistive network designs—they don't make sounds, like most people think; they actually just extend control over other areas. [MZ]

Used to be labeled *Angst*, *Regret*, and *Forgiveness*. Who changed my settings? [JT]

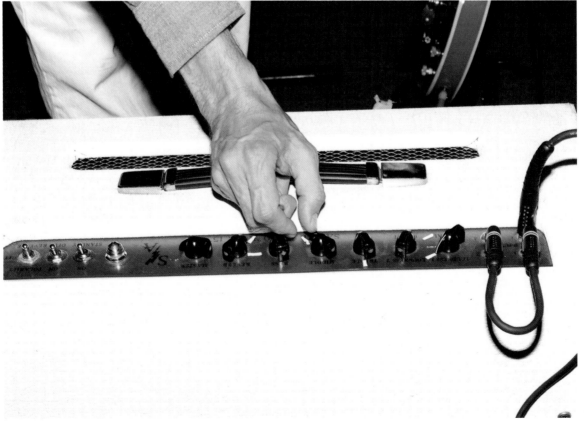

The main reason I think touring is really good is that it's really good—and good for you—to play music in front of people and to participate in bringing people together, sharing—and, on a good night, really connecting—with a bunch of people in a room all listening to the same thing. It's a really great thing to do. I don't think a band is completely viable unless they are actually a working band that plays. I'm not saying the records aren't viable, but the whole idea of a band to me is both. The traveling can be really exciting and beautiful, and you get to see so much stuff all the time. I tend to get worn down by it after two weeks, though.

At this point in my life, touring gives me a lot more structure than being at home does sometimes, because I know where I have to be at 5:00. There's a lot of anxiety that can come with coming home and transitioning back into this free-floating life. I really have to generate my own schedule to write. It requires discipline that I don't have sometimes.

There are days when I look back and hope that I learn how to enjoy the touring life more and more, because there are times when you feel like you've missed it somehow. Because it really is hectic, and I think what happens over time on a trip is that you start to conserve all your energy for the two hours you're going to be onstage. And so you miss a lot of sightseeing, or you don't do it at all. The irony is that you'd probably have more energy for the stage if you actually lived your life. But it's really tempting sometimes to go, *I can't do it. If I do that, I'm going to be tired on stage. It's the last thing I want.* [JT]

Each tour changes within the general parameters of what "touring" is. There is an emotional arc for each tour, and while it never configures itself in the same way, there are common elements that always manifest themselves. A few: 1) A great show. Everyone is clicking, and the gear and PA are behaving themselves. The music is as effortless and intuitive as I wish it could always be. 2) I've wound up (not by design) hosting the pre-tour hotel-room hang, and it's always a great way to start whatever round of touring we have coming up. 3) A long bus drive. There's usually one considerably long bus drive on any tour. This is more common on the west coast, i.e., Las Vegas to Denver, or Missoula to Seattle. These rides are a nice respite, especially when traveling through particularly scenic parts of the country. These drives tend to be in the eight-to-twelve–hour range, and the bus drivers usually take a two-to-three–hour nap in the middle of the trip. When possible, they'll find a mall or shopping center with restaurants, etc., so we'll be able to go eat and pick up necessities. Or, as is more often the case, non-necessities. 4) A rough show. Every tour has 'em, and the way to manage them is to review in your mind what went wrong and quickly move on. Dwelling on a bad show benefits everyone very little. [MJ]

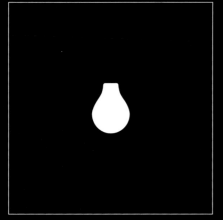 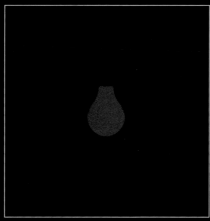

At times one can experience the image of an object "hanging" in one's perception for a moment after the light stimulus that caused it is gone. When one turns out a light, one can sometimes still see the image of the lamp for a moment in the darkness that follows. This appearance is called a positive afterimage. When differing images are projected onto the retina in very quick succession, images and afterimages mix optically to form new images.

A computer to lose its data
in the event of a power failure

A balloon to pop
A housefly's wings to beat one stroke

A honeybee's wings to beat one stroke
The sensation of toothache pain
to reach the brain of a cat

The amount of darkness following light
that is needed to complete the cycle
of photosynthesis

Most cameras to take a picture
(1,000 per minute)

Minimum time for an echo
to reach the human ear

The duration of a sixteenth note
if the metronome is set at 1/60

Minimum time for the human eye
to move from one point to another
and focus again

The duration of an eighth note
if the metronome is set at 1/60

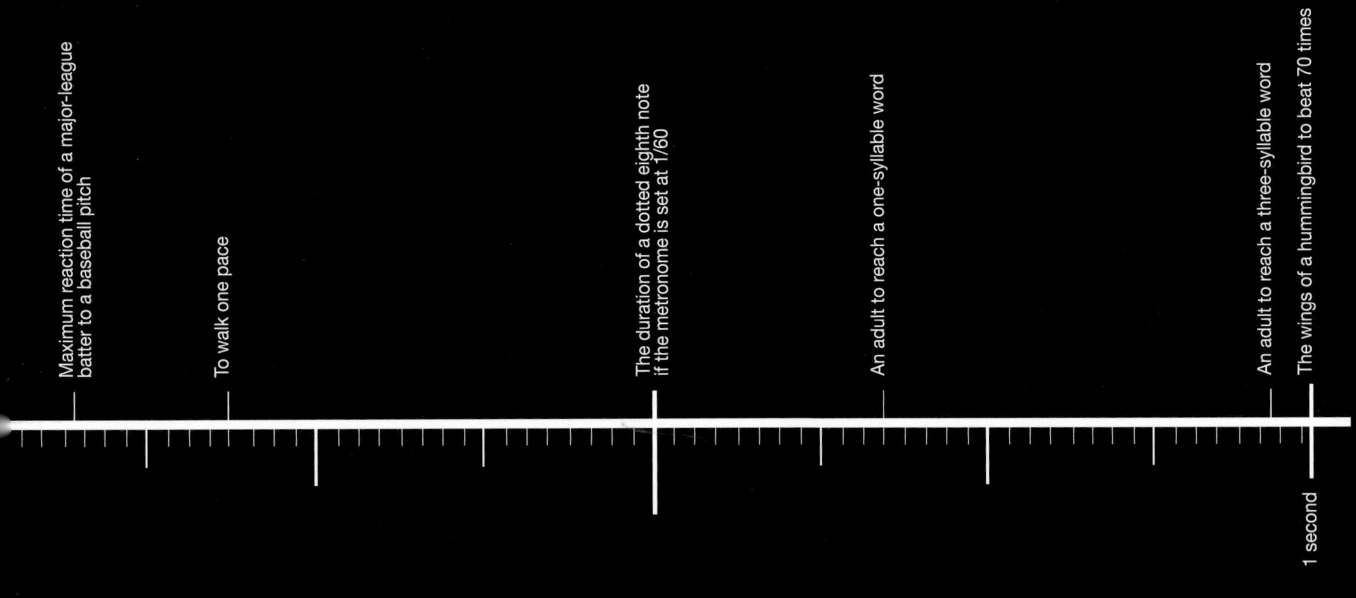

Maximum reaction time of a major-league
batter to a baseball pitch

To walk one pace

The duration of a dotted eighth note
if the metronome is set at 1/60

An adult to reach a one-syllable word

An adult to reach a three-syllable word

The wings of a hummingbird to beat 70 times

1 second

dBpm, a fake album cover painted by John Stirratt for a pre-A ghost is born recording session

I only want to make records that inspire me to want to make many more records, that open up a window onto a thousand different ways of putting together a record. [JT]

Making a Record

In November of 2003, after a lengthy tour and some starter sessions in Chicago, Wilco went to Sear Sound Recording Studios in New York to record the follow-up to *Yankee Hotel Foxtrot*, called *A ghost is born.*

WRITING:

I could make a lot of analogies to writing, but I don't know if they'd make any sense. Personally, I feel better when I'm making raw material—sketching stuff musically, writing things in notebooks, just accumulating. That's the pure stuff, the essence of everything, the stuff that comes from somewhere that you can identify as being *other than you.* You let it come out in the way it's supposed to come out, and look back later and maybe not remember anything about why it was written. The best stuff is smarter than you are, and it just doesn't smell like you.

As a band we try to nurture an environment where we do that together, too—make raw material. You're not going to write unless you have a pencil in your hand, so put a pencil in your hand. It's almost like practicing making music. As a band in the studio you put yourself in that environment and nurture that environment, and then allow freedom to exist, or stuff to just generate itself. Then something closer to craft comes into play, when you start trying to give a form to the raw material using skills you've accumulated over years of listening to music and shaping things. At the same time, there's another layer of creativity that happens at that stage that's more conceptual. It's impossible to generate something without also generating a conceptual receptacle sturdy enough to hold it—creating a big shape to put the little shapes in.

On *Yankee Hotel Foxtrot*, the big shape was America—write about America. The deeper part of that shape. I wanted to write about the stuff right in front of my eyes, microscopically looking at America, and asking questions about each little thing. *Is that really America? Is buying cigarettes and Coke evil, or is it just cigarettes and Coke? Is the cash machine evil, or is it blue?*

Since *Yankee Hotel Foxtrot* was finished, the world has changed, and my perception of the world has been forced to change in a very violent way, an extremely vicious, unsettling way. Like everybody's has. I am not a big fan of overtly political art. In the past, I've made the argument that all

Walter Sear of Sear Sound, with tuba (see Appendix IV)

hummingbird

his goal
had become
to be an echo
riding alone town after town
toll after toll
a fixed bayonet through the great southwest
to forget her

she would appear
in his dreams
and in his car but in his arms
she was everything
a cheap sunset on a television set could upset her
he never could...

his goal in life was
to be an echo
the type of sound that falls around and then back down like a feather
but in the deep chrome canyons
of the loudest manhattens no soul could hear him
or any thing...

~~near the end~~
he slept
in the mountains
in a sleeping bag underneath the stars
he would lie awake and count them
but the great fountain spray of the great milky way
~~wouldn't let him~~ never let him
die alone

(so he said)
remember to remember me
standing still
in your past
floating fast like a hummingbird
like a hummingbird
like a hummingbird
like a hummingbird

Things change so you can remember where you are. [JT]

art is political in the sense that the choice to make, rather than destroy, something is political enough for me. But that's not a satisfying enough rationale for me right now. There's so much deception and untruth—so many elaborately constructed façades that have become so empowered and bold. So I felt like I needed to at least move in a specific direction, to do more than only create.

I had a really strong impulse to not cater to any fantasies or deceptions in any way. The thought of making another really idealized record, like *Yankee Hotel Foxtrot*, where you can pretend that you're just making art, just making interesting shapes, just cutting stuff out, wasn't anywhere near as honest to me as living on a record and allowing it to be what it is. I wanted to confront people with an unreconstructed organic piece of art, alive in their ears. It felt very political to me in a way that no other record has ever felt, without it being very specific, or certainly without it being a sermon. I guess the ark concept kind of came out of that idea. What else can you do as one person making something? It's like, *oh well, at the very least I'm going to remind myself that I was here, and I was human.*

As a general guideline early on in writing material for *A ghost is born*, I wanted to avoid writing in the first person, and I wanted to try and avoid writing things that were so personal, just as a challenge to myself. And so I started writing from the points of view of animals—or at least impressions of animals. Over time, that led me to the idea that you could make a record as an ark—like Noah's Ark—and populate it with animals. That led me to the idea—just to broaden it a little bit—that all records are arks. All great works of art that end up meaning a lot to me over time, and can sustain long periods of rereading and still resonate, are arks in a way. Any one great work of art—you could build a universe worth living out of it, out of only its components. And I was thinking of how great records are exactly that to me—you take any great record and it contains everything that you need to know about music. And, hopefully, it contains enough ideas about freedom, and love, and spirit, about being human, that you can get an idea. That concept really structured how I thought about finishing the record and organizing it. I just decided to think of it as an ark and, *okay, say my children's children listened to this. Would they be able to reconstruct my worldview? What would they want to be on it?*

At some point, of course, I gave up on trying to make the record impersonal, because I think it was just an attempt to hide. And I realized that I just couldn't do it. I also realized that the third person doesn't really hide much. In fact, a lot of times, it's more naked because it shows the hand of someone trying to avoid himself. But by the same token, first person isn't always trustworthy either. One way I've tried to subvert the first person in the past is by using the Randy Newman idea of the unreliable narrator, which I like a lot. I've even written songs from the parts of me that aren't very trustworthy—or just the unsavory parts of my psyche, the things that I don't like to think about or talk about. To me, you can imagine anything, you can imagine murdering somebody. If you can't, you haven't watched TV. If you can't, you haven't really lived in our society. But what do you do with that? Do you keep submerging it? I don't know. I realized when I turned my mind off and just wrote, a lot of things like that would come out. Not dastardly things, but lyrics like *I dreamed about killing* and things. That's just what happens.

People take what they need from songs and leave out the rest of the story. Sometimes you want to spell everything out, but I've found that when I try to do that, I don't have much interest in singing those songs for very long. It's best if I've left enough windows or holes in it for myself so that the meaning can shift and I can integrate myself into it over time. The easiest way to do that is to be a really brutal editor, to pull out things that aren't just essence, to leave an impression of the original story—so that there's

different ways to shade it over time. It's like when you have your heart broken, and you turn on the radio, and every song is about you specifically, and your situation. I love that, I love that humans do that. We look for that structure and can identify it. I don't know if you can really consciously try and construct those open spaces, but you have to leave those holes there, as opposed to filling them and making the story airtight. Like "Muzzle of Bees"—it's very, very direct in some ways. There's a very specific message on an answering machine. The rest of it seems to be almost simultaneous—like having one or two lines that just poke out and speak in a direct way and crack the façade enough for the listener to be aware that there's a consciousness on the other end of it—like "I've been puking." Just so they realize that it's not just a bunch of words, and it's not just a disembodied voice—you can feel a consciousness lurking under there.

In the end, you make this record, put all these ideas into it, and accept it. And accept that it's hard playing, and unschooled, and romantic, and passionate. Accept that you cried making it. I can't listen to "At Least That's What You Said," when the music comes in, when the drums come in, without crying. It sounds like a panic attack to me. It's representational, you know. The second half of the solo when the guitar becomes more frantic is unsettling to me in a really beautiful way. It says more than anything I've ever written lyrically, and it just happened.

Those are the things that we really couldn't have *made* happen but were hoping *would* happen if we had faith in our process. It's an awful lot of highfalutin shit to say about a rock record. But that means the world to me. It's pretentious—that's the word for it. But I don't know of anything that isn't based on pretense. [JT]

In my opinion, this band is based around the lyrics. I relate to Jeff's lyrics the same as anyone else would, I guess: I find excitement and beauty in his images and combinations of words, and can appreciate them strictly on the level of the musicality of the language and freshness of the images. However, I also interpret them through my eyes and ears and let them take on a meaning that may not be even close to what Jeff has in mind. But that's what I think most fans do—once he releases the lyrics, they're as much everyone else's as his own, and our interpretations of those lyrics are as valid as his actual meaning. I'm pretty sure he agrees with that idea. Of course, since I'm on the inside, sometimes I have a clearer idea of what his meaning is—and that's cool, too, because on some songs I do want us to read them exactly the same so our musical interpretation/accompaniment is in concert.

Giving the lyrics real musical meaning depends on the song or the record. The musical process starts with just being aware of the lyrics and the way Jeff phrases or colors them in his vocals. That's what I tried to do on *A ghost is born*—just listen to the phrasing and inflections of his vocals and make the drumming as sympathetic and supportive of that as possible. Basically being in tune with each other and everyone else too—listening. On *Yankee Hotel Foxtrot* I was more concerned with making this imaginary place or percussive landscape for the lyrics to live in, giving them an environment rich with rhythm and fresh sounds and letting that environment evolve and react to the lyrics. That was more of a *sounds* record to me, and *ghost* is more of a musicianship record. [GK]

I was probably most aware of the *A ghost is born* lyrics because of how process-intensive the record was, but often I get wrapped up in the music and forget about the specifics. I've always been in collaborative bands—playing other people's tunes. You just hope they're good. And then being a part of delivering these songs live can be a really singular experience—it's Jeff speaking to the audience, but I'm part of the delivery and I feel responsible for the tone of it. [JS]

I don't really listen to the lyrics as much as I intuit their rhythm and feeling. It's something that I've struggled with for a long time. The music of a song, nine times out of ten, is what grabs me first. I'll usually come around to the lyrics around listen fifteen (or show forty!). It's a strange situation, to be in this band. Even though I cowrote two of the songs on *ghost*, it's ultimately

It's very simple, what you look for in an engineer. You look for a human being who is self-confident enough and sure enough of his skills to not have to put his mark on stuff. Basically, you look for transparency. Problems come about when someone has an ego and wants to say, "But *my* name's going on this too." The simplest way to put it is you look for an engineer that is okay with coming out, listening to the sound you're actually making, and putting a microphone in front of it, and then when you walk back in the control room after he's recorded it, it sounds like the sounds you were making. [JT]

Jeff's vision. My ideas meshed well with what he was trying to achieve, and that's that. I'm fortunate to be in a position to offer my musical ideas in a venue where they're invited and thoughtfully considered. However, Jeff is such a driven individual and follows his concepts to whichever end they need to get to (in his eyes), it can be frustrating and exciting all at the same time. I have a feeling that it's a lack of confidence on my part; Jeff's been doing this professionally for a much longer time than I have, has many more experiences in the studio, has been performing for much longer than I have. So all of that makes me censor myself more than I should. Each record is finite, and there's always the next Wilco record to work this stuff out with/on. [MJ]

PHILOSOPHIES OF ART AND RECORDING:

At this point in my life I value a lot of art that talks about itself. I value art that manipulates how I approach other things. But, at the same time, I do feel compelled to back away from a more formalist idea of art because I'm really suspect of the idea that there's ever been a fully realized piece of art. I don't think that I've ever made a fully realized piece of art. I've always felt like the best stuff within anything I've made has been the stuff that I didn't intend to be there, that I look at and say, how did that happen? That's the stuff that makes it worthwhile to me. Because if you could imagine it, why do it? Why take that journey? [JT]

There has to be a reason to make a record—an idea behind it. For this record, it wasn't really a verbal thing, we just understood. A lot of it between Jeff and me isn't verbal. We just understand each other. A lot of it, for me, was empathizing with what Jeff saw and relating to it as though I were in a parallel storyline. My records are thematically very similar to what Jeff does, even though I do it differently than he does. The theme isn't negative, per se, it's more like a description of the negative—it's trying to articulate a way out of it.

To get somewhere, you have to take a car. But the journey isn't about the car; it's about the destination. Those narrative devices he uses are like the car. My car is different than his, but we generally go to the same place. We understand each other that way. I see a lot of the subject matter on the record as the car. I can't really articulate the destination—it's too elusive. Werner Herzog talks about ecstatic truth—it's going for that real thing, the un-grabbable thing. That's the thing about any art form: it's the elements of that particular medium that are unique to it that are able to articulate things that no other medium can. That's what makes that work so special. It's all about knowing whatever it is you want to communicate. You may know what it means, but the challenge is to find a way to communicate that meaning to other people. It's not like you're trying to dumb it down, because you're trying to find a new way to say it for yourself, too. You have to. [JO]

PRODUCING:

I think that a good recording, on a physical level, should leave space where you can hear into it, can hear depth. It should not be just a wall of sound—an impenetrable, monolithic thing. A lot of modern recordings are only that. Even Phil Spector's Wall of Sound is deceptive in that way—it's so roomy. [JT]

The final focus of any recording session has to be the song. At one point, the bigger concept for *A ghost is born* was that there would be bigger arrangements that would be all set when they got to New York. If there were strings, they'd be in the room with the band; if there were horns, they'd be there. And everything was going to be recorded live. We wound up not needing that stuff, but kept the idea of everything being recorded in a room together—a lot of rehearsing, a lot of jamming. For the first chunk of time at Sear Sound, we just played. Most of the time, if there was a mistake we'd stop and do the song over. And it wasn't about getting the exact best sound—which is another reason why I was there, because an engineer might try to over-fix the sound. I argued against the use of any synths and stuff. I didn't want any. It's not my record, but that was part of my devil's-advocate role. I want to hear the air around things. To me, synths and things like that are too vacuum packed. The air is everything. The song that benefited the most from that approach was "Wishful Thinking."

I don't like music that's about musicianship, about being able to technically play your instrument. That's something I really watched out for on this record. Every note has to matter. And it has to deal with time and form. Pacing is so important to what I want in music. That's what's it all about in mixing. You tear apart songs, and stretch out parts, and make them work for the pacing. But this record was from the ground up—we were always looking at the pacing. Whatever I do is always about pacing. It's what makes sense to me. I don't like stuff that's just on and then off. Other kinds of music work great for that, but not songs. Songs, to me, are like storytelling. I don't like any playing that draws attention to itself—I don't like individual parts that say, "Look at me!" It's not about that; it's about working together towards a destination. Every song has a different destination. Pacing is the foundation; without it, you're not carried along, there's nowhere for you to go. You sit outside of it, and it goes through the motions, and it's over. If it's done right, you've gone from point A to point B.

The sound has to have character. If I could relate this record to any other, it would be *If I Could Only Remember My Name* by David Crosby. That record has a community sense, of everyone working for a bigger goal. That record has these hotshot players on it, but it's all toward something else. That record has some transcendent moments on it, like "Laughing." And the Bill Fay records are huge, too. Their sense of urgency remains an inspiration. [JO]

Early, half-serious, thematic diagram by Jeff Tweedy for *A ghost is born*

SEAR SOUND AND RECORDING:

The biggest change for me at Sear Sound was that I didn't have to engineer, as I did when we recorded at Soma over the last couple of years. At Sear Sound I was able to focus solely on playing with the band. The old engineer/band member dual role became really tricky after a while, when my place in the band became firmer and firmer, and there were songs that I was architecturally a part of, rather than overdubbed on, so there were a lot of times when I had to hit *play* or hit *record*, and then run out, play and let the tape go, and then come back and have to sort through it all, having not been able to adjust levels or get a rough mix going during the performance. Somehow we managed. But I was very relieved not having to do all that in New York, and just play.

Walter Sear, the studio's namesake, has been in the business forever. He's always around. He doesn't do sessions, but he's doing something. I never really could figure it out. It's funny because when we were there, he was like, "I don't want people calling these things vintage. I bought them when they were new." And it is a world-class gathering of some of the greatest microphones that have been made in the last half-century. It's the difference between good and great, good and amazing. It's that last—it's like most processes—that last little push, that last nine yards.

We were all set up in the live room where we tracked, and we tracked most of the stuff, if not all of it, with everybody in the open air without headphones. And just trying to play and hear each other that way. The box we had at Soma for headphones was four channels and stereo. At Sear Sound, it's sixteen and two stereo, so it's another level of things to get distracted with—*oh, I have control over that, I have to turn it down*—then you remove yourself from the song. So I tried to not use the headphones as much as possible. And it was fantastic. I mean, most of the time, you have to use headphones in overdubs, obviously, because you have to hear. One of the problems we experienced was having the bass low enough that it wasn't going to bleed into everything in a way that was going to be a problem. We had to manage the system of what's acceptable and what's going to be a problem, sort of address it as it comes up. So, one of the things we did to combat that bass problem was use a device called a thumper, which is a speaker driver that just attaches to a drum stool, so there's no actual cone involved, it's just transmitting low-end. When anybody would play the bass, Glenn would feel it in the drum seat, so that way they could, without having the volume play, be really in tune and in sync with each other. It's a standard rock thing. Glenn will probably end up using it live, and just having his kick drum go into that, so we don't have to have his monitor so loud. So that's one of those creative solutions.

Jim occupied a classic producer's role with this record. He'd say, "Yep, that's a good take," "That's not a good take," "I trust your vision," "Let's stick to it, guys"—like a cheerleader. Sometimes, "Ah, no, I think you guys could do better." *Yankee Hotel Foxtrot* was much different. That was very much a collaboration in taking all this raw material and trying to figure out how we could make it sound relevant, vital, and exciting, and give it a shape that wasn't as static as it had been. It was a weirder record before, but it was much more static. [JT]

Sear Sound is probably the studio that's closest to the Wilco philosophy of how to make records. The thing I've learned in this band is the value of things that have fewer knobs. For example, Jeff has an amp called a Stu Pro: all it is is one knob. It clicks on, to turn the power on, and then it's volume and that's it. But it's the greatest-sounding little amp of all time. And you could labor over pedals and signal processing to achieve a similar goal, or you could just get the thing that works and is great. And Sear has that kind of similar utility. Maybe it's not straight down the middle that way, but for the most part, this is the stuff that when it was designed, it was designed with these concerns, and if you use it properly, it will work without any help. Basically, the philosophy is *use the best thing on the best thing*.

I know for me, not using any technology on this record was really important, as a general rule—and using keyboards and the piano, and stuff that was designed with an inherent character, rather than trying to coax a sound out of something that can do a million things. You wind up having more of a relationship with the simpler instrument precisely because it's so obstinate. Because the piano, as versatile as it is, is not an organ, is not an analog synthesizer. It does what it does beautifully, and I use an acoustic piano on a lot of stuff, which is a texture that you can't—at least up until now—fully emulate with an electronic version. I always think of this concept of purity when it comes to an instrument. Was it conceived purely, rather than being a Swiss Army knife? Which is what I end up having to use live—because I need to generate all these sounds and it's just impractical for us financially right now to tour with a grand piano, a Hammond B3, a Wurlitzer, and any number of analog synthesizers. It's just unfortunate that we can't do it. Maybe down the road it will be possible.

The problem—the reason that we don't—is maintenance. In the '70s, it was probably a lot easier to find guys who could fix and tune a Wurlitzer and a Hammond B3, but those guys are numbered. It's

something I battle all the time, because I have to play a piano through an amplifier, and it sucks: you just do the best you can with the materials and the resources that you have. But man, I'll tell you, it's not cool to be a keyboard player. It's not a social instrument like the guitar, where you can just bring your guitar backstage and play some songs. I was doing it—I have a little keyboard on tour, and I had a little amp—but it's just so frustrating because you always wind up dealing with the parameters and the levels. With a guitar, you can just have somebody string it. But then there are things that I'm able to do that you can't really achieve on the guitar. The actual range of the instrument is greater than the guitar. Not that it's me against the guitar player, but it's really great as a tool to create a texture that's complementary to the guitar.

Some of our most compelling performances have been radio shows where we had a really stripped-down setup, where it's just Jeff on acoustic, Leroy on piano, me with a keyboard, John on bass, and Glenn on a really small, stripped-down drum kit. And the performances were really great, even without all of the *Yankee Hotel Foxtrot* effects, the bells and whistles. Obviously, that's a testament to the songwriting, but it's also a testament to the fact that we can pull it off, that we don't need all that—well, not that we don't need it, but it's another avenue to take with these songs. And I think the Fundamentals (see Appendix I) process informed this as well—the live chance. And it's a challenge for all of us. It was terrifying for me—you don't want to be the one who makes a mistake during the take. But then, after a while, there was stuff that happened that I thought was a mistake, and that was when they'd go, "Man, that's such a wrong chord. No, wait, that was good, we should do it again." [MJ]

MIXING:

A lot of mixing is arranging, like plotting out a scene. A song has to have that kind of structure. I'm not into music for music's sake. What is needed? What serves the song best? The lyrics and the song: that's what it's about, not individual parts. Just because something's been recorded doesn't mean it has to be used.

A lot of it is pacing it out. And it's like rewriting scenes, you go through different arrangements and parts, where they've been and where they are. A lot of it is going through it again and again until it feels right as a song and in the context of the whole record. I think of it like lighting, blocking the lens; not literally, but in a sense I see it like making a

film. Apparently, when I'm mixing—or so Jeff says—I rub my thumb and index fingers together. I'm not sure I believe him. I do, however, make mad dashes for equipment. If I get an idea, I've got to do it. Eventually the other guys would stay on the other ends of the desk, because it was like a crazy man coming through. I see what it is, and I see what's needed. It's just that feeling. I know technically what I need to translate to get that, but I don't think of it that way. We're not building an airplane. I think most people don't sit down and listen to records with real concentration. If they did, they'd be so rewarded. There are so many more layers of stuff that are considered. Jeff and I both know. There's a reason for the song, and there's a reason for the way it's mixed. [JO]

MASTERING:

Mastering is getting all the tracks to their appropriate levels. Everything as loud as it can be, without distortion, then a little bit of equalizing to make it all level. And a little bit of voodoo. [MJ]

8

1 The question before us is about the nature of evolution. The question before us is whether evolution, generally speaking, is smooth and proceeds at a certain rate, or whether this evolutionary business is full of abruptness and complexity, such that its rate is not fixed, nor its surface smooth. The question before us is whether the evolution of a certain kind of composition, a composition that looks on the surface as though it might be erratic and violent, is in fact more orderly than it appears. Or perhaps the question is whether a surface that appears relatively smooth and consistent can be, on its obverse, mottled and disorderly. The question before us, a question whose response herein has five parts, is whether a thing can be itself and be its opposite at the same time,

Five Songs

Illustrations by Wilco

and whether a composition can intentionally embody an ambition and its opposite, and, if so, what this means for one attempting to apprehend or interpret this composition, as in the case of a listener attempting to get comfortable with some music.

The first release by the band called Wilco is called *A.M.*, and since the release has the picture of a radio on the front cover, it would be reasonable to assume that the record alludes to the AM band of American radio, the music technology of the childhood of the members of Wilco. In the New York metro area, the AM radio band, and thus popular music, was controlled by WABC radio and WNBC radio, and by disc jockeys like Cousin Brucie Morrow and Harry Harrison. Does *A.M.* allude to deejays of this kind? Deejays who used too much reverb on their broadcasts, and who always talked over the beginnings and endings of songs? Does the A.M. of Wilco's title refer to this tender and nostalgic AM radio of our youth? Is the album's relatively *sunny* and *twangy* means of expression a reflection of this radio of our youth? Or is it not possible that A.M. suggests something else entirely? What if A.M. alludes to the transmission, in 1900, over a distance of one mile, of the words "One, two, three, four. Is it snowing where you are, Mr. Thiessen? If it is, telegraph back and let me know" by one Reginald Aubrey Fessenden? Does the A.M. of Wilco's title refer to this primitive AM band? Or maybe, notwithstanding the photograph of the radio, is it not possible that we are instead referring here to A.M. as in *ante meridiem*, otherwise known as *before noon*, and thus is it correct to conclude that *A.M.* has the intention of being sunny and twangy—which it arguably is, on songs like "I Must Be High" and "Casino Queen" and "Passenger Side"—or are we more exactly speaking of a *morning* of composition, which is to say a *new day*, like the *new morning* of another folk-rock troubadour? No, perhaps *ante meridiem* goes too far as an interpretation, except that no interpretation goes too far with Wilco, even on *A.M.*, because its very simplicity is also deceitful and ambiguous. Take, for example, the beautiful "I

Thought I Held You," which contains the lines "I'm like a songwriter / You're the reason I've run out / Run out of metaphors." Meaning what exactly? Is the writer of the song *not* a songwriter? How can he be "like a songwriter" making use of the similitude of "like," when he *is* in fact a songwriter, the lines themselves serving as the proof? And when he says he has "run out" the first time, does he not mean "run out" as in abandoned, as in ended a *love relationship* (if you accept the prevailing interpretation, perhaps the narrator is alluding to having *ended a band*), such that he is both ending a love relationship and "running out" of or exhausting his metaphors (metaphors being somewhat different from similes), or is he simply extending a line so that it scans properly, so that it fits into the space allotted?

When the beautiful "I Thought I Held You" moves forward from its desperate similes, it moves forward into a chorus, which I would argue is written in direct address from the failed songwriter (*I'm like a songwriter, so I'm not a songwriter, but rather someone who is attempting to use simile as though I were*) to the audience, who might think that this sunny and twangy song is just what it appears, sunny and twangy, when what it actually is something altogether more desperate: "I don't even think you understand / I thought I held you by the hand / I thought I held you." Which means what exactly? Does it mean the failed songwriter is abandoning a love relationship, or ending a band? Or is it rather a very desperate and harrowing question about whether this endeavor, the endeavor of songwriting and band-making, the routine of writing, recording, and touring, is actually connecting songwriter and audience at all? Are you actually getting the meaning I'm attempting to send to you, in this failed system of transmission, the popular song, or is the system somehow faulty? And if it is faulty, with what shall we replace it?

For the purposes of a discussion of evolution, however, I didn't mean to talk about "I Thought I Held You," though like almost all of *A.M.* it is, in its way, perfect. Rather, I meant to speak about the strangest and most out-of-place song on *A.M.*, the song called "Dash 7," which is not sunny at all, and though it has the ubiquitous pedal-steel guitar of *A.M.*, the kind of thing that folk-rock zealots manage to turn into a cliché that must appear on all records in order to insure legitimacy, it doesn't *sound* like it has a pedal steel. Because the song does not capitulate to the one-four-five-with-relative-minors song structures that make *A.M.* so easy on the ears ("Can you keep it simple? / Can you let the snare crack?"). Instead, "Dash 7" makes use of a modal tuning and some passing chords as a way to get at some really acute loneliness, like so much of the later and more self-evidently complex work by the band known as Wilco. Therefore, "Dash 7" appears to prefigure this evolution of which we speak. What "Dash 7" does is go from a one-four (D to G) progression to b minor, and then to emphasize the possibility of a C chord, a half step up from B minor. It's a passing C, a diminished C triad with a suspended second, if it works the way it sounds, which is a chord that would sound a little challenging to some

Jason Tobias, *Las Vegas by Bus*

rock-and-roll ears. And because it's difficult, it's evolutionary.

However, the question before us, with "Dash 7," is *What is the song* about? Is the song really about a certain kind of propeller plane, one in the transport category, first manufactured in 1975, popular in Europe, discontinued in 1984, after a mere hundred of the planes were built? (Lately, the Dash 7 has been used by the U.S. Army for surveillance.) Because of the slipstream around the prop, the Dash 7 is known for *firm* landings, which are not necessarily easy on passengers, and "Dash 7" the song seems to take on the matter of the Dash 7 in the moment of landing. Yes, songs about touring are well known, lamentations about touring, and at first glance, "Dash 7" would seem to allude to the endless travel of a musician's life: "Dash 7 in the air / Propped to the sun alone / Jets hum / I wish that I was still there / Props, not a jet, alone / Where the sun doesn't come down." Sure, it's probably just a song about touring. That would be obvious. At least until the chorus: "Because I've found the way those engines sound / Will make you kiss the ground / When you touch down." Is "Dash 7" about the way the engines sound, in general, or about the possibility of engine failure, the possibility of calamity, and is the captain's announcement in the third verse ("Dash 7 pointed down / The captain's announcement / Doesn't make a sound") an intimation of *bad news*, and is its soundlessness part of a strategy to create in the listener a certain kind of *audition*, as John Cage called it? Because, without giving up its mysteries, "Dash 7" fades into twenty-five seconds of looped rumbling—apparently

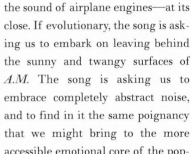

the sound of airplane engines—at its close. If evolutionary, the song is asking us to embark on leaving behind the sunny and twangy surfaces of *A.M.* The song is asking us to embrace completely abstract noise, and to find in it the same poignancy that we might bring to the more accessible emotional core of the popular song. Indeed, the later and more complex work of Wilco tries very hard at discouraging passive listening, and the pristine, ominous, and melancholy "Dash 7" begins this transition from sunny and twangy, even as it establishes a reputation for same, by first composing an old-timey melody about the sound of plane engines, and then including looped industrial noise at the melody's close.

Oh yeah, and while I was thinking about "Dash 7," I happened upon the following: The first execution in the electric chair involved a gentleman called Kemmler, who converted on death row, who repented before the current flowed, thus: "I want only to say that a great deal has been said about me that is untrue. I am bad enough. It is cruel to make me out worse." In order to prepare to execute Kemmler, an audience of electricians had to test the technology on an animal, a dog convicted of biting, a dog who first required three hundred volts, and then four hundred volts, and then seven hundred volts and who still would not die, who tore his muzzle and menaced the crowd, and the name of that dog was Dash.

2 Beneath the sunny and twangy surface of *A.M.* is something else, and I have been trying to point in the direction of this something else. Our job is to divine what Wilco is trying to say, in these five fathoms down. Does supplemental material indicate the *obverse* of whatever is indicated in the exterior of *A.M.*? The situation is like unto the voice of Jeff Tweedy. Like the memorable blues and gospel singers, like Charley Patton or Son House, Tweedy's instrument has a gravelly overtone (partly owing to his consumption of the demon tobacco, no doubt). His voice is parched in that way that Westerberg's was back when he was a Replacement. And yet Tweedy sings beautifully. His is a voice of yearning, loss, dry wit, occasional rage, and impatience, and almost none of these colors is obvious. What Tweedy appears to be saying with his instrument is almost always as evident in silences and hoarse passages as it is in the sung melodies. Here, it seems obvious that the manifest content of the instrument is not the true or entire content. And yet neither is a specific subtextual undercurrent being conveyed. What is being conveyed in Tweedy's voice, and perhaps in the *sprawling* and *ambitious* song cycle known as *Being There*, is discontinuity: between surface and subtextual intention, an intention, even on its own, that is very difficult to articulate.

"Misunderstood" is a popular song on the second album recorded by Wilco, entitled *Being There*. It's sort of an anthem, in fact, and "Misunderstood" would

John Stirratt, *The Barracuda*

seem to be the correct song to write about in order to understand the evolutionary movement of the band called Wilco, because "Misunderstood" happens to be *about* rock and roll in some ways. It also seems to be about the success of *A.M.* and the kind of expectations that an audience might have for the compositions of the album that follows. Remember that this album is named for a story by Jerzy Kosinski that concerns a simple-minded gardener called Chance who inadvertently becomes a political hero by blurting out homely lines about trees and shrubs. Remember that the album also quotes from a song by Peter Laughner, he of the early demise from liver damage, he of the famous Rocket from the Tombs: "Take the guitar player for a ride / Because he ain't never been satisfied / Thinks he owes some kind of debt / It'll be years before he gets over it."

Evidently, there are interesting spots here where an interpreter might gain purchase, as when a climber ascends sheer rock face. We have the fine punk-rock wailing at the beginning and the end of "Misunderstood," which is played well in concert, in footage I have seen, etc. I admit the importance of the line "You look honest when you're telling a lie," which is in the category of paradoxical statements that ultimately become ubiquitous in the ongoing Wilco project (see, e.g., *Yankee Hotel Foxtrot*, for more discussion of same). Similarly, here we have the accusatory second person that is actually a first person (used to fine effect by Elvis Costello). All these reasons are exactly why I am *not* going to write about "Misunderstood," because "Misunderstood" is trying harder than it needs to. Its anthemic quality is premeditated, which is in some respects true of the whole of *Being There*.

Instead, I am going to offer the hypothesis that *Being There* is about more than being misunderstood, although it does pass through that *topos*. It is about *not* being *here*; it is about being in part absent from the creative process in one fundamental way, it is about recognizing that beneath what is *here* is a completely different address, a wormhole, a trembling ocean of ceaseless movement, viz., the unconscious, erupting at all places and at all times, in "Dreamer in My Dreams," for example, and in "(Was I) In Your Dreams," and "Outtasite (Outta Mind)"—all of them, to some extent, about the pressure of unseen worries and unseen registers of consciousness on a love relationship, about this recognition that things are going on beyond the perceptual capabilities of the ordinary senses. It's everywhere on *Being There*—the desperation to figure out how to deal with *crisis*—the crisis of success, perhaps, but also some more chronic discomfort, some chthonic discomfort, this discomfort best summed up in the beautiful and obsessive "Sunken Treasure," a song that does exactly what it claims it's *not* going to do.

"Sunken Treasure" contains the line "There is no sunken treasure," as if attempting to deny the existence of the subliminal layers of composition, as if to strike a blow for a materialist reading of human experience. And it then goes on to chart much of its course in ambiguous figures of speech, e.g., "If I had a boat / You know I'd probably roll over," plunging in the process into the sea—a terrifying occurrence, as any seafarer will tell you, whereupon this seafarer will need to *turtle* the craft, in the formlessness of the ocean; remember, for example, Pip in *Moby-Dick*, who falls out of the longboat, is left for several hours, and, when plucked from the sea, has lost his wits. The immensity of what's under the surface of the sea is what is terrifying; as Juan Eduardo Cirlot remarks, it is a "vast expanse dreaming its own dreams and asleep in its own reality, yet containing within itself the seeds of its antitheses." Oceanic anxiety, chthonic anxiety— also apparent in the "rows and rows of houses" in the first verse of "Sunken Treasure," with their television lamps running "parallel to you," the listener, into which lurches this noise of sunken treasure, the sound of timpanis, multiple electric guitars, much piano banging, all of it overtaking the lovely simple melody of the verses, just as in "Misunderstood," which opens the other disc. Here, with a more terrifying intention, is music attempting to convey what can't be spoken (cf., "Outtasite": "I know we don't talk much…"), attempting to summon the unspeakable, and when Tweedy gets to the out chorus on "Sunken Treasure," it is less to say that he resents the audience or is conflicted about his place in the business of rock and roll than to say how the popular song has written its history *on* him and *in* him: "I was maimed by rock and roll / I was tamed by rock and roll / I got my name from rock and roll." As in orthodox Catholic theology, Tweedy is *with* his idiom, and he is *in* his idiom, and he is *through* his idiom, and it has inscribed itself on him, and this is a recognition of the multiplicities and complexities in this sprawling and ambitious album, which takes the estrangement of "Dash 7" and blows its ambiguity up into a nearly symphonic scale— breaking with the safety of *A.M.* while observing the principle of discontinuity.

3 One of the oldest English-language jokes, according to a teacher I had in college, is one we learn in the first phase of language development. *Q: When is a door not a door? A: When it's ajar.* What does it mean for a door to be ajar? It means that the ability to contain information and systems of meaning is in a state of eclipse; *ajar* stands for *threshold*, *ajar* stands for the fact that in churches the doorway is always farthest from the altar, and thus, the door is the antithesis of the system of meaning contained in the altar. And that makes perfect sense on the way to discussing the *moody* and *ambiguous* album called *Summerteeth*, whose apparently tuneful first song nonetheless contains the lines "No love's as random / As God's love / I can't stand it" and "Your prayers will never be answered again," while Jay Bennett's electric-piano solo tinkles merrily in the background. *Door* goes back to Middle English, *door* goes back to Old High

German, goes back to Latin and Greek, goes back to Sanskrit, which means it is among the oldest of words, as *church* is likewise, deriving from the Sanskrit *sura*, which brings us to *ajar*, which comes from the Old Norse *kjarr*, which brings us, on *Summerteeth*, to the song entitled "She's a Jar." It's impossible not to come to this song, as one comes to this album as a whole, with a sort of stunned feeling about the lyrics. I am not, of course, saying that the lyrics were not plenty good on the first two Wilco releases. They were good for rock and roll. They were unassuming, and charming, and frequently funny. And yet on *Summerteeth*, it's like the lyrics *want to get somewhere*, and the somewhere is really anguished, and really ambitious, and really beautiful.

It's my assumption that domestic life at some point becomes a factor in the Wilco biography, as with all rock-and-roll bands. The practitioners of rock and roll begin to age, and in the process of aging, they begin to run afoul of some of the hallmarks of the rock-and-roll life—traveling, fickle attentions of fans, etc. One can assume that in Wilco, more permanent attachments, such as marriage and children, began to intrude. (This is evident, for example, in the film about Wilco, which depicts Jeff Tweedy in completely tender moments with family and children.)

The advent of this domestic arrangement begins to intrude on the lyrics of the band; the responsibilities of family, as opposed to just *being in a love relationship*, are here, on the moody and ambiguous *Summerteeth*. "I'm worried / I'm always in love" is the matrix sentence for the album, as the theorist Michael Riffaterre might have put it, the red-hot center, the still point. On the other hand, what about: "I dreamed about killing you again last night / And it felt all right to me"? Far from repudiating or explaining this line, Tweedy, newly ambitious lyricist, has volunteered to attest to the intensity of this observation. Self-evidently, it is the lyric of a conflicted participant in the domestic process. And since we are talking about dreams, as we have been above, let me point out that

last night, I myself dreamed of Wilco. Like this: I was invited to watch the band play in Chicago, and they were playing at some bar, as they apparently had been for weeks, and first I sat down with Tweedy and we did some Q&A, and Tweedy claimed that the reason that he didn't want to play the *conventional popular song* anymore was that it had *too many whole notes* in it. To prove the point, Tweedy actually wrote out, on a napkin, several measures of a popular song, scribbling whole notes for several measures. Other members of the band joined the discussion, and yet soon they were instead accusing someone—not anyone actually *in* the band called Wilco—of diluting the power of the music by *fucking groupies*. This stranger was fired on the spot by bass player John Stirratt.

Yes, the song from *Summerteeth* to which I want to draw your attention is "She's a Jar," which is a woebegone and beautiful ballad, such as one might not have been surprised to hear on the early Wilco albums, except for the orchestral palette, which now includes synthesizer—or is it chamberlain or mellotron? Similarly ornamented is a really big bridge and chorus, a soaring chorus, in which the narrator "floats above the people underneath." This being more evidence of the anxious apartness of *Summerteeth*: "Please beware the quiet front yard," or "When I forget how to talk I sing," or "My face gets sick / Stuck / Like a question unposed." These lines admix with fervent affections like "She's a jar / With heavy lid / My pop-quiz kid." A sense of isolation *should* be resolved when the domestic question is resolved, and yet somehow this disparity is *not* resolved on *Summerteeth*. The interrogatives pile up violently here. The lyrics are just as unsettled as the arrangements on this calliope album, the first without pedal steel and violin, the first with Brill Building passing chords written in here and there. It's an album that wants to get somewhere, and that doesn't mind if it sacrifices some *No Depression* music fans in the process. *Summerteeth* says *Yes, Depression!* The somewhere it wants to get is perhaps into the terrain of the early Velvet Underground, as in the end of "She's a Jar," wherein the protagonist says of his lover, "You know she begs me not to hit her," which recalls the Velvets' line "You better hit her" (from "There She Goes Again").

Whereas one might actually believe in Lou Reed hitting someone, or at least one believes in Lou Reed's ability to observe someone who might hit his or her girlfriend, one feels considerable doubt about Jeff Tweedy, sensitive guy, panic-attack sufferer, hitting anyone, but that is what you get on *Summerteeth*, you get sweet melodies accompanying fierce and rather troubling lyrics. Which is what you should get on a transitional album. Which is to say that *Summerteeth* is the album that precedes the unearthly *Yankee Hotel Foxtrot*, and as such, at first glance it seems inexplicable. I remember finding it inexplicable when I first heard it. I remember thinking, *What is it with this record?*, loving it and not understanding it in equal measure. Because where was the pedal steel, but, also, what to make of these

Jeff Tweedy, age 8

lyrics? Because these are not lyrics that trust in the confessional, unless what is being confessed is doubt about the efficacy of confession. *Summerteeth* feels like the door to the refuge has gone ajar, and you can see in long focus into the church interior, and you know how long a sprint that's going to be when you try to make the dash for the spotlight.

4 *Yankee Hotel Foxtrot*, album of Chicago. Chicago is the place it was made, the place it was *filmed*, and Chicago is the musical environment in which its profound perfume of failure begins to smell like success. *Yankee Hotel Foxtrot* is lead made into gold. Drummer got laid off, guitarist got laid off, label rejected the record, another label repurchased it, album went top fifteen, etc. We have heard these kinds of stories, and these kinds of stories are very satisfying. But is there a way to get beneath the surface of the publicist's breathless excitement, to get to what is going on beneath? Because *Yankee Hotel Foxtrot* is the triumph that does not give away its secrets immediately.

Chicago. As symbolized by the lopsided photograph of the Marina Towers on the front cover. I remember seeing the Marina Towers the first time I was in the Windy City. There's some great architecture in downtown Chicago, some of the best architecture in the country, in fact. The Marina Towers are not examples of this great architecture. The Merchandise Mart, e.g., just a few blocks away, is much more beautiful. The Marina Towers are an early example, I believe, of cast concrete, from a period in which there was a vogue for

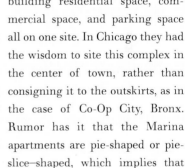

building residential space, commercial space, and parking space all on one site. In Chicago they had the wisdom to site this complex in the center of town, rather than consigning it to the outskirts, as in the case of Co-Op City, Bronx. Rumor has it that the Marina apartments are pie-shaped or pie-slice–shaped, which implies that they are hard to decorate. What do you put at the point of the apartment? The Marina Towers are not attractive from a classical standpoint, but they are American, like vinyl tablecloths or corncob holders, which are actually sort of what the Marina Towers resemble: corncob holders. While management denies it, local residents believe that the towers really *are* tilting. Thus, the lopsided photo on the cover of *Yankee Hotel Foxtrot* looks genuine, not stylized.

This is not the Chicago of Wicker Park, where Liz Phair famously lived. This is not the Chicago of tastemakers, but the Chicago of Americana, where America happens, and yet this Americana is given a bizarre twist on the *cerebral* and *affectionate* album called *Yankee Hotel Foxtrot*, and you can tell this right from the beginning, because "I Am Trying to Break Your Heart" opens with a droning onslaught of noise, synthesizers, xylophone, autoharp, guitar feedback, and then abecedarian lyrics—lyrics that are at first *about* the letter "a" and the things that might be done with this letter, followed by some alliteration involving "b," and "c," etc.: "I am an American aquarium drinker / I assassin down the avenue / I'm hiding out in the big city blinking / What was I thinking when I let go of you." What does this mean, exactly? Unfortunately, *Yankee Hotel Foxtrot* does not encourage questions like *What does this mean?* Perhaps even the purveyors of *Yankee Hotel Foxtrot* know not what these lyrics *mean*, which indicates, arguably, that we are working in a context of automatic meanings or chance procedures: "I want to hold you in the bible black predawn / You're quite a quiet domino bury me now." As a lyrical approach, of course, this certainly is miles from "Casino Queen," "Passenger Side," and the other early Wilco songs. As an approach, it doesn't sound that far from the stuff happening in Chicago, if by Chicago, we mean the Drag City/Thrill Jockey aesthetics of Jim O'Rourke, David Grubbs, Tortoise, The Sea and Cake, et al. Even the songs that are more conventionally structured, like "Kamera," and "Heavy Metal Drummer," where the chord structures are not completely unknown to the rock-and-roll hordes, even in these songs we find hints of a kind of experimental ringing and droning.

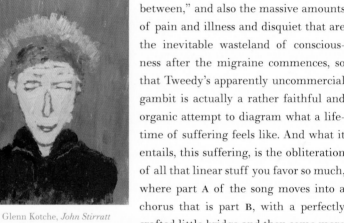

Glenn Kotche, *John Stirratt*

On the relatively summery melodies, there are lyrical allusions to darkness and disorder: "Phone my family and tell them I'm lost on the sidewalk" or "There is something wrong with me" or "How can I convince you it's me I don't like?" Love songs, if that's what they are, that are all about doubt, including an entire song about having reservations about the idea of love. And there are the epistemological obsessions we found on the prior two albums: "All my lies are always wishes" or "It's beautiful to lie." What to say about *Yankee Hotel Foxtrot*, but that it is deeply disturbed and masterful. So faultlessly produced that it makes indie rock, whatever that once was, sound orchestral, in terms of its scale, it makes post-rock sing, makes roots music sound like electronica, and it does so while, in my view, perfectly describing a migraine.

Indeed, Jeff Tweedy's lifelong struggle with migraine seems to be *the* generator of themes on *Yankee Hotel Foxtrot*. You can see the spots where the auras begin their blossoming everywhere: "My mind is filled with silvery stuff," and "You could be my demon moving forward through flaming doors," and "You were right about the stars / Each one is a setting sun," and "All I can see is black and white and white and pink with blades of blue that lay between," and also the massive amounts of pain and illness and disquiet that are the inevitable wasteland of consciousness after the migraine commences, so that Tweedy's apparently uncommercial gambit is actually a rather faithful and organic attempt to diagram what a lifetime of suffering feels like. And what it entails, this suffering, is the obliteration of all that linear stuff you favor so much, where part A of the song moves into a chorus that is part B, with a perfectly crafted little bridge and then some more of part A and part B. All of that goes into the compactor, and what remains there is the huge implacable monolith of *pain*. Admittedly, sometimes Wilco *tries* to work the love-song stuff in around the migraines.

There are any number of songs that indicate the purity of this cerebral and affectionate album. I was, initially, completely infatuated with "Radio Cure," which is morbid and almost clinically depressed, until it gets to the B section, when it sounds chipper and upbeat while repeating over and over the line "Distance has no way of making love understandable." But in fact, "Radio Cure," with its migrainous observations ("There is something wrong with me /

My mind is filled with radio cures / Electronic surgical words") is too simple as an emblem for *Yankee Hotel Foxtrot*.

No, the irrefutable masterpiece on this album of masterpieces is actually "Ashes of American Flags." Therefore, it's best to concentrate here. The title alone requires exegesis. Of course, *ashes* are what the alchemists had as their end-stage byproduct, and *Yankee Hotel Foxtrot* is not without imagery of conflagration elsewhere. There is also in these ashes an evocation of the prehistory of contemporary Chicago, a city that has so much good architecture in part because it was burned to the ground. This was in 1871, and they'd had twenty fires the previous week. That's how dry it was. The fire jumped the Chicago river at one point, burned down the opera house, the courthouse, etc. It's as if an earlier idea of Wilco actually needed to be *incinerated* in order to get to this recording.

Another layer of the title would seem, at least to this listener, to allude to the perennial time-waster of congressional Republicans, the flag-burning amendment to the United States Constitution. The last major legislative push in this direction was in 2000, notwithstanding failures in 1989 and 1990 and 1995. While it's fair to say that the lyricist of *Yankee Hotel Foxtrot*, roiling in his migrainous anguish, is unlikely to write a song *about* the flag-burning amendment, he certainly has an afterimage from the 2000 senatorial debate close at hand, as he also seems to hear Mrs. O'Leary's cow lowing sweetly.

"Ashes of American Flags" commences with its own little chamber-music drone, and then we have the one four five, and we have the singer and his reification of contemporary Chicago, built on the ashes of the old: cash machines, Coca-Cola, and cigarettes. This leads him into a brief invocation of the meaning of poetry, then his usual epistemological anxieties about lying. At which point the rhythm section drops out, and there is the droning of electronic effects, echo-laden electric guitar, and from there we are at the summit of this heartbreaking song: "I'm down on my

hands and knees / Every time the doorbell rings." Reminding this listener of the famous description of Nathaniel Hawthorne—that he was given to fleeing into the woods when in danger of passing anyone on the road. Not a bad gloss for a narrator who ends his ditty thus: "I would like to salute the ashes of American flags / And all the falling leaves filling up shopping bags." The conjunction being between the material of everyday life in Chicago (ATMs and cigarettes) and the residue implicit in ash and dead leaves.

The course of the album and the progress of the band follow the alchemical model implicit in "Ashes of American Flags." *Yankee Hotel Foxtrot*, then, is a record of what must be incinerated to be perfected, namely all popular music, so that the cerebral part, the heroic-investigation part, the troubadour part, may flourish. This process of incineration gets to why this is the perfect Wilco record, so far, and why it is not the album with the most *hits*. Whatever those are. The album recognizes explicitly what was implicit on *Summerteeth*, namely that there is animus lurking under the domestic fulfillment of the popular song, there is disgust, there is despair, there is suffering, and in the grip of this animus, there is desire again, always the recirculation between the two, disaffiliation and desire, the yearning for the happily-ever-after popular song. The thing and its obverse. *Yankee Hotel Foxtrot*, with its wall of noise, recognizes this paradox, takes what has been implicit in the earlier Wilco albums, just offstage, and brings it into the spotlight—brings it, in fact, into the mix, where complexity becomes self-evident, as a style, as a methodology, as a sound.

5 The resource that is required for the just assessment of popular music is *adequate time*. Or, the mistake of criticism in this attention-deficit–disordered age is twofold: lack of space and lack of time. Never enough space is devoted to criticism and never enough time is given to the premeditation of this analysis. Nevertheless, this essay, in attempting to both conclude and remain timely as to the evolution of the

band called Wilco, now attempts a hasty response to *new* work by Wilco, which is the recently issued recording entitled *A ghost is born*, and yet this essay does so with the idea that evolution at the instant of its transformation always looks more like mutation. Still, let it be said that *A ghost is born*, in haste, is *post-historical*—as Arthur Danto has said of Andy Warhol's soup cans—in that it means to follow an album that was the end of all possible albums. What sort of art do we make after the internal imperatives of a form have been exhausted? The answer being: *Anything you want.* After history is liberty. And so we have *A ghost is born*, with its fluxion of styles and ambitions, some Brill Building, some stuff that sounds like gospel, some long-lost tracks from *Music from Big Pink*, some punk rock, some post-rock, and so forth. *Post-historical* and *liberated.* Free from the burden of which Stephen Dedalus spoke: "History is a nightmare from which I am trying to awake."

Certain tendencies may in this instant appear to be features of post-historical endeavor. Simplification may appear to be a feature. For *A ghost is born* seems to want to repeal some of the sonic palette of *Yankee Hotel Foxtrot*, it wants less electronica, less digital flourishing, less Pro Tools, less synthesis, less lead-guitar playing (of the traditional sort). It wants more analog, more ensemble playing, more spontaneity, more raw discovery. It wants more ache in the singer's voice. As *Yankee Hotel Foxtrot* toyed with drones, *A ghost is born* toys with silences. Mostly here the drones are live instruments, not digital signals. Post-historical endeavor also continues to favor a song structure that is looser and more arbitrary, part A of the song glued to part C, with part D attached in for a middle eight, and then never repeated. No part B at all. Yes, that *liberated* aspect of *Yankee Hotel Foxtrot* is expanded and enhanced. Yes, many of these songs, fresh from the oven, as I have heard them, feature beautiful sonic transitions, sudden violent metamorphoses from one section to another, because they *can*, because that's what one does with one's liberty.

The perceiving intelligence that sings out in this post-historical and liberated album has some things in common with the perceiving intelligence as described above, in songs one through four, e.g., discomfort, melancholy, a kneeling posture ("I got up off my hands and knees / To thank my lucky stars you're not me," e.g.), but it adds new leitmotifs to the oeuvre, viz., the *infernal latitudes*, common to two of the really beautiful ballads on this recording, "Hell Is Chrome" and "Wishful Thinking": "When the devil came / He was not red / He was chrome and he said / Come with me." Likewise, in "Wishful Thinking," we find "The turntable sizzles / The casting of spells / The pressure of devices / Hell in a nutshell / Is any song worth singing / If it doesn't help?" Hell, in a nutshell, is cast liberally around on *A ghost is born*. And any attempt to plot an optimistic and loving course out of the infernal regions here feels sweet and ambitious and doomed.

And yet, through these hellish latitudes *A ghost is born* also charts the progress of a new and engrossing insectile perspective. By the insectile perspective, I refer to the perspective that Richard Feynman described when metaphorizing about a universe with more than four dimensions. Imagine, Feynman argued, you're a water bug on the surface of a lake, born here on the surface, destined to die on the surface. Your perspective is confined to the two dimensions of lake on which you survive, for you are never going to be beneath the surface where the fish circumambulate, nor are you going to be soaring among the birds high above. How do you react, water skimmer, when a rock is thrown into the lake in front of you, and in the ensuing explosion you are cast up off the surface of the lake for the very first time, and you begin to see, as never before, that there is a whole way of thinking about the surface of the lake that you never before understood? This is the insectile perspective of *A ghost is born*, the bug made aware of his predicament, the citizen of four dimensions beginning to understand, for a fleeting instant, the possibility of *more*.

And perhaps it goes without saying that *A ghost is*

born was also recorded and released during a time of national crisis. The bugs, the insects, of *A ghost is born* are yearning for what is next, for what is possible now, for a way of seeing after disaster (as Tom Verlaine wrote, "I love disaster, and I love what comes after"), and a way of being in which the cataclysm of the rock falling into the lake and the disturbance of two-dimensionality is now ineluctably a part of their experience. "Hell Is Chrome," with its depiction of hell as a place of cleanliness, a place both "precise and towering," is a depiction of the time *after* cataclysm, a time of roiling ferment, as it is likewise a set of nautical charts for a region that exists outside of space and time. This is a place that simplifies your options, reduces them down to *certainties*, so that the "Come with me" of the chorus, repeated at length, suggests the woeful and faintly comical politics of hell, and this hell is about as mournful and beautiful and sad as anything that Wilco has ever recorded. This is the thing about the time after history: it is full of seductions ("Come with me"), the allure of certainty, and if you turn aside the Mephistophelean pact that is offered you, well, then everything is possible for you, *everything is possible*, and you are destined to be uncertain, sad, and scared. *A ghost is born*, at first glance, is like this liberty—vast, terrifying, intoxicating, true.

So these are the five songs with which to reckon: "Dash 7"; "Sunken Treasure"; "She's a Jar"; "Ashes of American Flags"; and "Hell Is Chrome." What do the songs tell us about how people mature, how songwriters grow up? What do the five songs tell us about evolution? Evolution always seems impossible, obscure. No wonder the creationists are confused. Do you ever *see* evolution take place? Can you watch natural selection in its flourishing? Can you watch a virus mutate?

Mikael Jorgensen, *The Osaka Skyline*

The same with artists and musicians. From a distance, the changes in an artist's life look violent. How does Picasso get from the Blue Period to high Cubism? What about Aaron Copland? There was all that Americana, and then later, some rather strident serial stylings. In popular song, there are the radical mutations in the work of a David Bowie or a Neil Young.

From the air, Wilco looks like a band that has metamorphosed at a great velocity, engulfing experimental impulses with each album, incorporating them swiftly, confidently, and intuitively. And yet, upon close inspection, it seems to me, the five songs here wrenched from their settings have quite a bit in common, beyond Jeff Tweedy's voice and a certain way of playing the acoustic guitar. The five songs have in common a way of looking at *meaning*. In the main, the popular song is a nugget of resolution, of encapsulation. Its material is amber. "California Girls" is about girls from California. "Let It Be" is about letting it be. Love songs explicate love, bring love's inexplicabilities in close where they can be *resisted*. But the five songs here don't do these things at all. These five songs, in each case, and taken as a whole, celebrate ambiguity and complexity and uncertainty without sacrificing deep feeling. They articulate the passions, but they don't simplify them. The five songs allow feelings to stay insoluble, as they are in life—perceptible, but insoluble. The five songs focus the lens on their narrators only briefly, after which these narrators are subdivided, or combined with other narrators, other perceptions, other contexts. And in this way the Wilco project, as shadowed forth here, seems more about *possibility* than about any other subject. The five songs are about the lust for possibility. Just as evolution itself is about the dynamism of possibility and change.

—*Rick Moody, December 2003*

9

Wilco (Footnotes),
Michael Schmelling

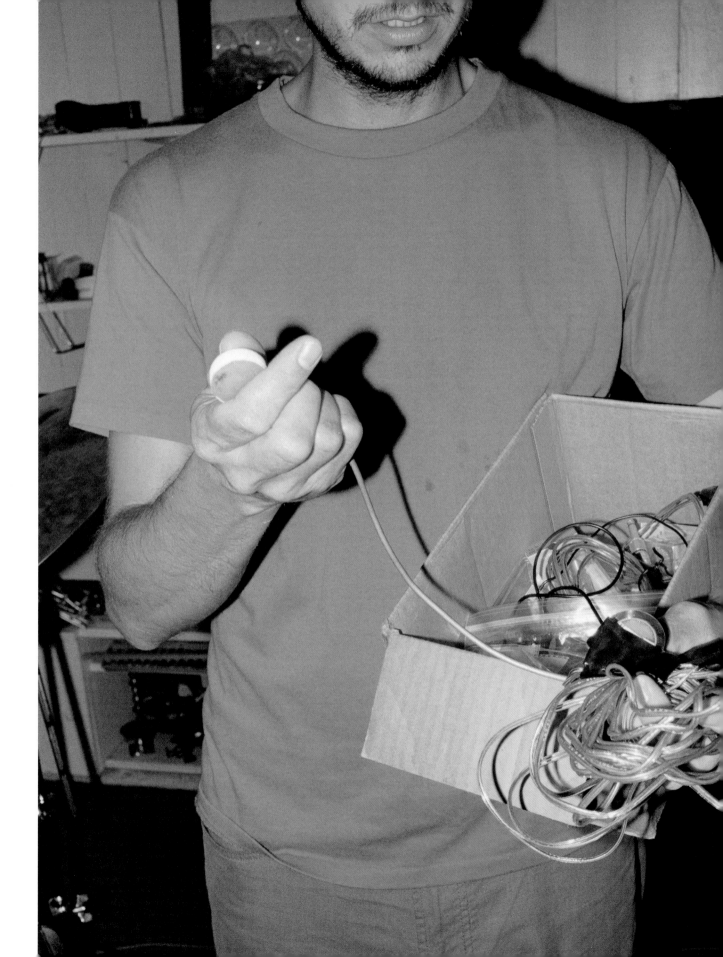

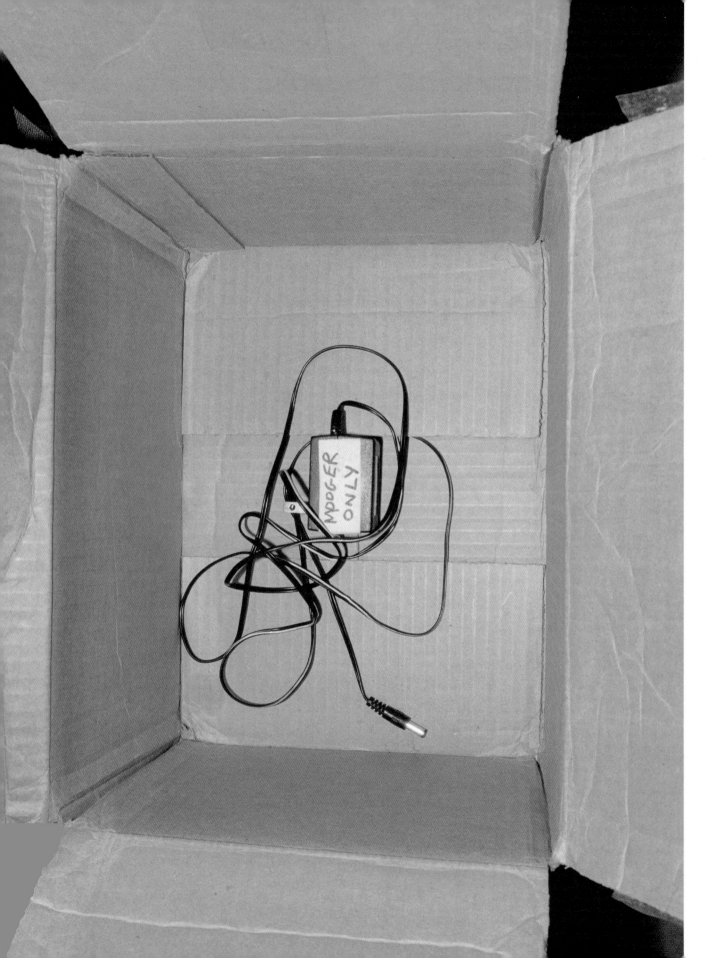

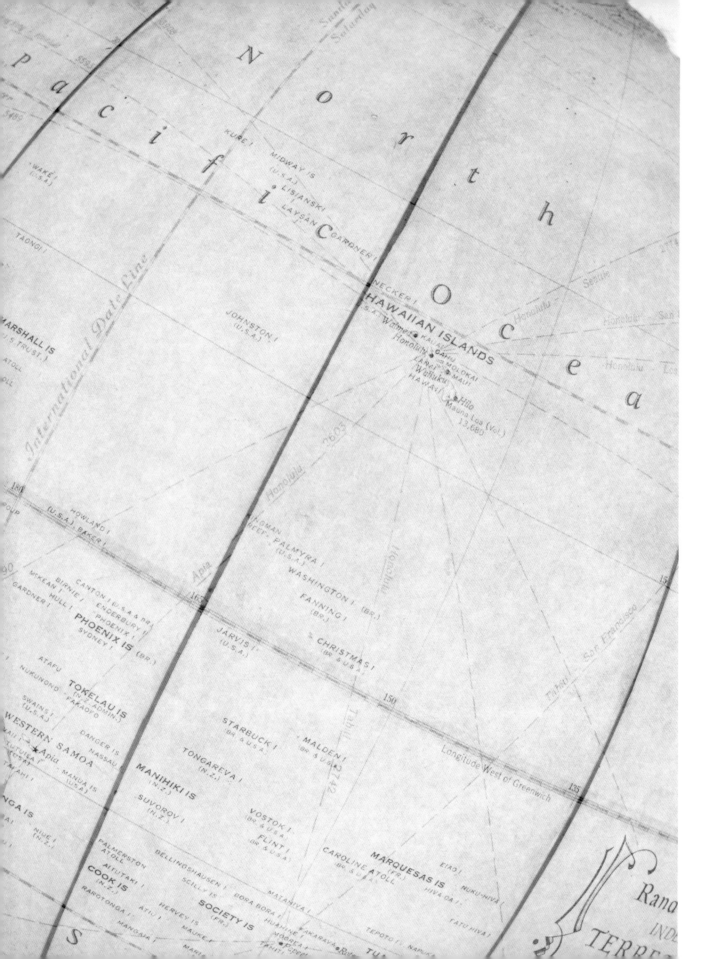

North Pacific Ocean

KURE I.
MIDWAY IS. (U.S.A.)
LISIANSKI I.
LAYSAN I.
GARDNER I.

WAKE I. (U.S.A.)

TAONGI I.

NECKER I.
HAWAIIAN ISLANDS
KAUAI
NIIHAU OAHU
Honolulu MOLOKAI
LANAI MAUI
Wailuku
HAWAII
Hilo
Mauna Loa (Vol.) 13,680

Honolulu
Honolulu
Honolulu
Honolulu

Seattle

San

JOHNSTON I. (U.S.A.)

MARSHALL IS. (U.S. TRUST.)
ATOLL

International Date Line

180

HOWLAND I. (U.S.A.) BAKER I.
GROUP

KINGMAN REEF PALMYRA I. (U.S.A.)
WASHINGTON I. (BR.)
FANNING I. (BR.)

Apia

165

CANTON I. (U.S.A. & BR.)
BIRNIE I. ENDERBURY I.
McKEAN I.
HULL I.
GARDNER I.
PHOENIX IS. (BR.)
SYDNEY I.

JARVIS I. (U.S.A.)
CHRISTMAS I. (BR. & U.S.A.)

ATAFU
NUKUNONO
TOKELAU IS. (N.Z. ADMIN.)
FAKAOFO
SWAINS I. (U.S.A.)
DANGER IS.
NASSAU I.

150

STARBUCK I. (BR. & U.S.A.)
MALDEN I. (BR. & U.S.A.)

Tahiti

Longitude West of Greenwich

135

WESTERN SAMOA
SAVAII Apia
TUTUILA I. (U.S.A.)
TAU I. MANUA IS. (U.S.A.)

MANIHIKI IS. (N.Z.)

TONGAREVA I. (N.Z.)

SUVOROV I. (N.Z.)

VOSTOK I. (BR. & U.S.A.)
FLINT I. (BR. & U.S.A.)

CAROLINE ATOLL (BR. & U.S.A.)

MARQUESAS IS. (FR.)
EIAO I.
NUKU-HIVA I.
HIVA OA I.

NGA IS.
NIUE I. (N.Z.)

PALMERSTON ATOLL
BELLINGSHAUSEN I.
AITUTAKI I. (N.Z.)
SCILLY IS.
BORA BORA
COOK IS. (N.Z.)
RAROTONGA I.
ATIU I. MATAIVA I.
HERVEY IS.
MANGAIA I.
MAUKE I.
SOCIETY IS. (FR.)
HUAHINE I. TAKAROA I.
MOOREA I.
TAHITI
TUAMOTU
FATU HIVA I.
TEPOTO I. NAPUKA I.

Rand
IND
TERRE

Appendix I: Liner Notes

When the band wasn't touring, Wilco spent 2002 and 2003 recording with a variety of agendas and ideas. The band switched from recording songs proper to doing conceptual improvisations, and back again, each approach feeding the other. As Jeff noted, "We were working on specific songs and doing the traditional kind of building tracks of recordings simultaneously. We'd get to the end of a normal recording day—having built tracks in the traditional way—and look at the clock. If it was, say, 10:00 p.m., and we'd planned to go 'til 1:00 a.m., we would decide to do an improvisation of some kind." Mikael Jorgensen began as an engineer for Wilco, but over the course of 2002, he gradually became a member of the band. Unless otherwise noted, all text below is by Jorgensen. The process was:

Improvisations: The first session, the so-called dBpm session (*dBpm* was also the working title of what became *ghost* while we were recording the "proper" tracks at Soma Electronic Music Studios), was only six days long. At the end of each day we'd have a conceptual practice led by a different member of the band. Each improv had varying degrees of structure and/or instructions. They were referred to as improvs because the actual music being played or sound produced was not written or preconceived: it was up to each player within the parameters of the given "director's" instructions.

Deadlines: This was an attempt to simply play music together for thirty minutes or so and look at it like a live show or set. I wasn't a member at this point, so I was simply recording. For me it was a way to get sounds and levels really quickly. Once everyone started playing, I'd leave the knobs alone (during a song), because it's better to have a great take with a consistent level and perhaps compromise some fidelity than to burn out musicians by optimizing every parameter while they go through the song over and over again.

Fundamentals: A recording scenario where Jeff played in the live room with just an acoustic guitar and a notebook or two of lyrics, and Glenn was in the isolation room playing drums or MiniDisc. Leroy, John, and I were in the control room playing synths and laptop. We'd usually play until the reel ran out, so about twenty-five–plus minutes. Using the headphone monitoring system at Soma, the following "rules" were used: *1) Jeff can only hear himself and/or Glenn. 2) The four of us were able to hear everyone. 3) Do whatever you want.* Then I'd set up the CD-R to record the playback, and Jeff would mix the whole twenty-five or thirty minutes or so on the fly, so the mixes themselves became another level of performance and interpretation. There were about seven of these sessions. Something has made me very curious lately about the Fundamentals sessions. After listening to the first few that we did, it all just sounded like ingredients. The individual sessions were hard to keep straight in my head, and I regrettably wound up not listening to them all that often. On tour somewhere Jeff asked us all to come listen to one of them in the back lounge of the bus. That's when it changed for me. I had been listening to it unmusically. Once I heard it as something so teeming with subconscious ideas, it all made sense. We all fantasized about doing a Fundamentals tour where we would've had similar workstations and recreated one of the reels of tape, note for note. Clearly, that was never going to happen, and thank god. However, the freedom and the ability to simply create and react as mindlessly as possible was the education.

I called Deadlines "rehearsing making a record in real time." The challenge was to make a record in the time it would take to listen to it. I'd turn off my mind to the idea that you can't make a record in real time and then say, *well, what would come next if I was listening to this?* [JT]

All of these sessions were an attempt to try new things as a band and to get to know each other in different musical settings. We wanted to just be a band and not necessarily worry about making *a record*. We recorded them because any of them could have possibly ended up being part of or all of, or inspiration for, the next record. I consider the entire process—dBpm, Improvisations, Fundamentals, Deadlines, and the New York sessions—part of *A ghost is born*. To me, that's why the end of "Less Than You Think" is on *ghost*: it's a part of Wilco and should have every right to be on the final record (even though it sounds more like the improvs than the rest of the final *ghost* songs). *Ghost* would not sound the way it does unless we went through all of those processes to see what resonated with us and what direction/sound the record would ultimately have. We named them different things because they all had individual concepts behind them. But if you look past the names it's one very long process with detours and excursions along the way. [GK]

06. Here Comes Everybody [Fundamentals]
Recorded August 2002, Soma EMS, Chicago
Jeff — Acoustic Guitar / John — Synthesizers / Glenn — Drums / Leroy — Synthesizers / Mike — Laptop & Synthesizers

The musical theme in this song runs throughout the Fundamentals approach. There are several versions of this theme recorded, and this was one of the most compelling.

07. Hummingbird [*A ghost is born* contender]
Recorded February 2002, Soma EMS, Chicago
Jeff — Acoustic Guitar & Vocal / John — Bass / Leroy — Piano, Organ, Synthesizer & Percussion / Glenn — Drums, Percussion & Hammered Dulcimer / Mike — Mix

Ah, "Hummingbird." This was the third Wilco song I recorded. It was at this session that after each proper song was recorded, each member would devise an improvisation piece and "direct" the band appropriately. I was given three executive decisions that would be honored absolutely. At just under seven days, this was a relatively short session, and on something like day four, the guys had to go do an all-day photo shoot. So instead of sitting around and waiting, I told them that my first executive decision would be that while they were out at the photo shoot, I would mix the version of "Hummingbird" that they had recorded the day before. My second decision was to ban Jeff from playing slap bass in the control room. My third has yet to be determined. So I guess this is the part where I talk about the fact that I had been working on techno records leading up to this session, which explains why the kick drum is so godawfully loud. Nevertheless, I'm still a big fan of this mix. Glenn has always referred to this moment as being important to him. They all liked the mix, and I guess it worked, because here I am talking about it, and it feels like ancient history.

08. The High Heat [*A ghost is born* contender]
Recorded February 2002, Soma EMS, Chicago
Jeff — Acoustic Guitar & Vocals / John — Bass & Piano / Leroy — Piano, Organ & Synthesizers / Glenn — Drums & Percussion

This was the first Wilco song that I recorded. I was pretty nervous and was working at an extremely accelerated pace. This particular drum sound isn't my favorite; it's rather unsophisticated. However, the feel and atmosphere of the tune trumps any technical issues that I have. Working on this song was quite fascinating, once I got over my jitters. The guys recorded a traditional version of it: acoustic guitar, vocals, bass, organ, and drums. Leroy then put this super-out piano shit down and we muted the acoustic guitar, and that transformed it from a folksy-type number into what is on this CD. Fun.

09. Doubt [Fundamentals]
Recorded August 2002, Soma EMS, Chicago
Jeff — Acoustic Guitar / John — Synthesizers / Leroy — Organ & Synthesizer / Glenn — Drums / Mike — Laptop

With the Fundamentals process, transitions between songs became little events unto themselves. Some were more musical than others, and there were a few that were unlistenable. This particular transition sounds really terrifying to me, and hence its inclusion on this CD.

10. Barnyard Pimp [Fundamentals]
Recorded August 2002, Soma EMS, Chicago
Jeff — Electric Guitar / John — Synthesizers, then Bass / Leroy — Organ & Synthesizer / Glenn — Drums & Percussion / Mike — Synthesizers, then second Guitar

Here's a song from one of the later Fundamentals sessions. This was a bit different as Jeff was simply playing electric guitar in the live room and not singing. After the tape started rolling, I thought that the sanctity of the live room where Jeff was playing needed to be invaded. Fifteen minutes or so into the reel, John and I broke into the live room and began playing along with a song we (and Jeff) didn't know. This is the song where the invasion occurred. The awful out-of-tune guitar is all my fault. This track segues into an excerpt from a back-lounge jam recorded on tour somewhere between Ann Arbor, Michigan, and Columbus, Ohio, October 2002. With us on this particular trip, playing fiddle, was the magnificent Jim Becker of Califone, who were touring with us at the time. Jeff was on acoustic guitar, Leroy, Glenn, and I were handling percussion. I remember drunkenly trying to set up the laptop and some mikes with which to record what was happening, only to be stumped by it for reasons I can't remember. So I used

The Songs:

01. Pure Bug Beauty [*A ghost is born* contender]
Recorded March 2003 at Soma EMS, Chicago
John Stirratt — Bass / Leroy Bach — Piano / Glenn Kotche — Drums, Hammered Dulcimer & Percussion / Mikael Jorgensen — Mix

Working on the computer has its advantages every now and then. Using the digital audio multitrack program Pro Tools, it's easy to audition something at half speed. It's something I do from time to time while working on a song, and more often than not it just sounds like the song slowed down. In this case, however, there were elements that we recorded that wouldn't make it onto the final album version that, when configured in a certain way, gave this song an entirely different dimension. This version has always been a favorite of mine, but however much I thoroughly enjoyed mixing and listening to it, I knew it wouldn't make it onto the album. The last song on *Yankee Hotel Foxtrot*, "Reservations," employs the same "trick," as it were. After the (proper) song is finished, a half-speed version follows, with some embellishments.

02. This Is New [Fundamentals]
Recorded August 2002 at Soma EMS, Chicago
Jeff Tweedy — Acoustic Guitar & Vocals / John — Synthesizer / Leroy — Organ & Synthesizer / Glenn — Drums & Percussion / Mike — Laptop & Modular Synthesizer

This is an excerpt from the Fundamentals sessions of the summer of 2002. This was Jeff in the live room with just an acoustic guitar, lyrics, and a shitload of EMT Plate reverb, while Glenn was in an isolation booth, and John, Leroy, and I were in the control room reacting to what Jeff was playing. We could all choose to hear Jeff, but he couldn't hear us. Chance experiments met with wonderful consequence.

03. Diamond Claw [*A ghost is born* contender]
Recorded July 2003 at Soma EMS, Chicago
Jeff — Electric Guitar / John — Electric Guitar / Leroy — Bass / Glenn — Drums / Mike — Piano

This is the second recorded version of this song that we did for this record. Technically and musically, this is my favorite piece of recorded sound that came out of the sessions for *A ghost is born*. After some frustrating days grappling with another song, we all sat down after dinner one night in the tracking room and started playing this song. Since we were in mid-session, many microphones were still set up, so I ran into the control room, hit *record* on the computer, and just let the levels be what they were going to be. Since we didn't have to worry about tape running out, we just sat there and played through several different versions of the song, then went into the control room and picked the best one. I am very proud of this "terrible recording."

04. This Is New (The Explanation)
More from the "This Is New" session.

05. What Good Am I [field recording]
Recorded February 2003, Jeff's hotel room, Perth, Australia
Jeff — Vocals / Leroy — Guitar / Mike — Laptop

Leroy and I had spent a day on Rottnest Island, in the Indian Ocean, on the western shore of Australia, and we returned to our hotel in the early evening. Our rooms were adjacent to each other, so I had Jeff to my left and Stan on my right. On the other side of Jeff's room was Leroy, so after we got home and showered, stepping out onto the balcony, it was easy to see who was home and who wasn't. Jeff invited us to come to his room and record an album. So we got some wine and beer and headed over. I was messing around on my computer with some fancyish sample-playback thingy, Leroy was playing acoustic guitar, and Jeff sang, drummed, and rhythmically opened and closed the sliding glass door. I'm afraid "What Good Am I" doesn't feature the threshold-riding stylings of J. Tweedy, but it certainly reminds me of that evening.

the built-in microphone on my laptop, which has the same fidelity as a telephone, and pressed record. After recording about twenty minutes' worth of jamming, we listened back to it using the speakers on my laptop. The recording was a distorted trebly roar. I remember saying something to the effect of *This digital recording technology really sounds fantastic!*

11. Rottnest [Fundamentals]
Recorded August 2002, Soma EMS, Chicago
Leroy — Piano / Mike — Laptop

This duet happened at the very end of a Fundamentals session. Jeff had finished playing and singing, and he walked into the control room and sat down. I had stumbled upon this beautiful laptop texture close to the end of Jeff's last song and decided to let the tape run. Leroy ran into the live room and played this beautiful piano stuff over it, picked up only by the acoustic-guitar and vocal mikes. I like to think of this as a sweet goodbye to my good friend Leroy.

12. Hamami [Improv]
Recorded June 2002 at Soma EMS, Chicago
Jeff, John, Leroy, Glenn & Mike — Percussion

When Glenn was traveling in Turkey, he went to a serious Turkish bath, and in this cavernous space every little sonic event had this magnificent reverb tail. Water drops, doors closing, footsteps, etc. The idea was to emulate the chance sounds and see how it turned out with the addition of the human hand. We each had a surface to which a contact microphone was applied, and about six objects to drop onto this surface over the course of three minutes or so. The objects ranged from screws and beads to coins and chunks of metal. Some of the surfaces were drum shells, the floor, boards, and so on. Everyone had to play independently of each other and drop their objects at the pace of their choice.

A contact microphone is different than a traditional microphone in that it picks up physical vibrations transmitted through solid matter rather than through air. The benefit of using a contact mike is that there is much less potential for feedback because the transducer is contacting a surface. For example, you could affix a contact mike to the body of an acoustic guitar and get sound that way; however, if you remove it, you won't get a signal, or at least it'll be very, very quiet.

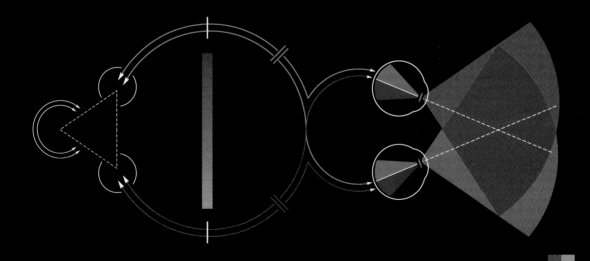

All songs produced and written by Wilco

Mastered by Dan Stout at Colossal Mastering

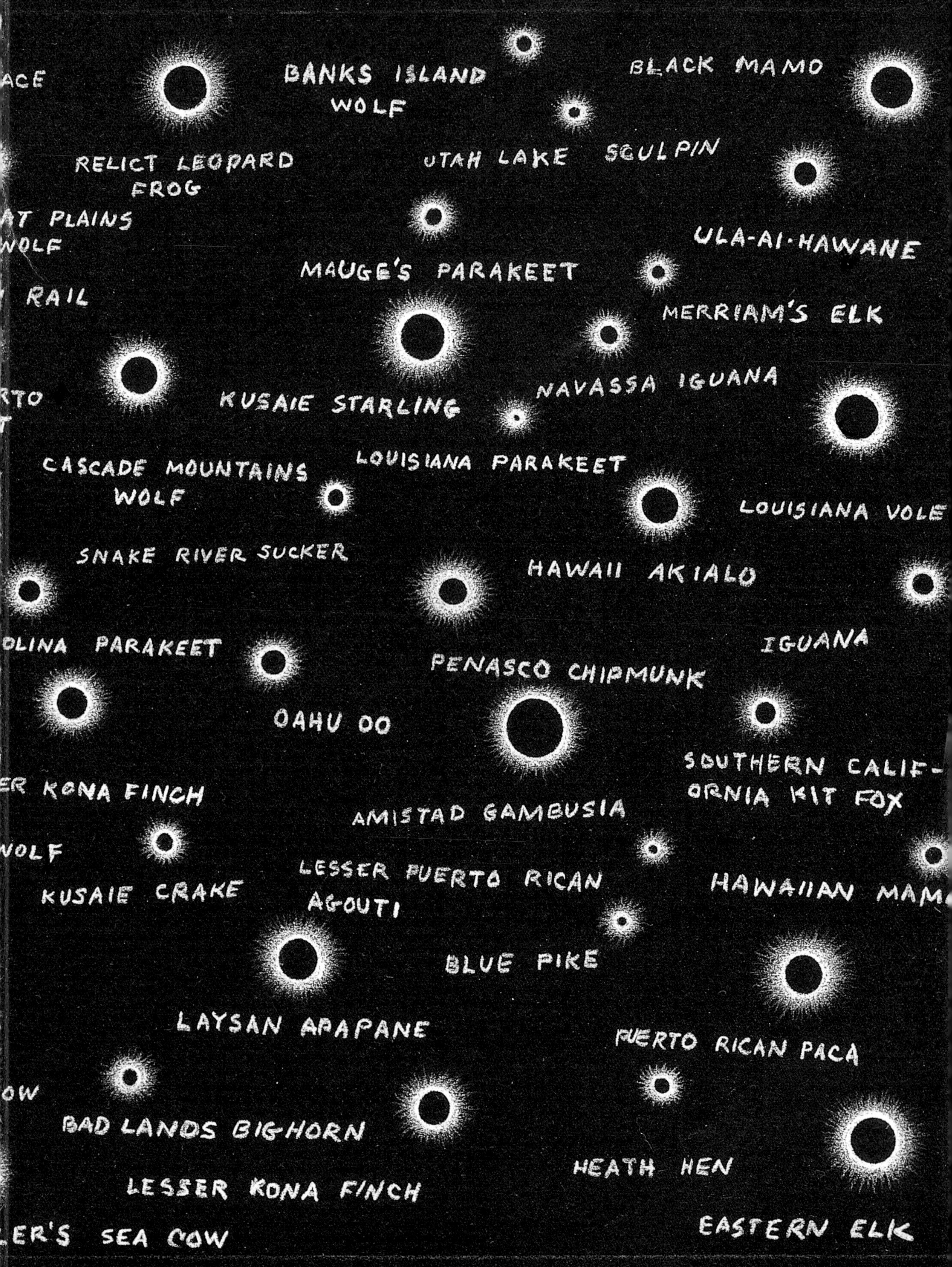

ACE

BANKS ISLAND
WOLF

BLACK MAMO

RELICT LEOPARD
FROG

UTAH LAKE SCULPIN

AT PLAINS
WOLF

ULA-AI-HAWANE

MAUGE'S PARAKEET

RAIL

MERRIAM'S ELK

RTO

KUSAIE STARLING

NAVASSA IGUANA

CASCADE MOUNTAINS
WOLF

LOUISIANA PARAKEET

LOUISIANA VOLE

SNAKE RIVER SUCKER

HAWAII AKIALO

OLINA PARAKEET

IGUANA

PENASCO CHIPMUNK

OAHU OO

SOUTHERN CALIF-
ORNIA KIT FOX

ER KONA FINCH

AMISTAD GAMBUSIA

WOLF

LESSER PUERTO RICAN
AGOUTI

HAWAIIAN MAM

KUSAIE CRAKE

BLUE PIKE

LAYSAN APAPANE

PUERTO RICAN PACA

OW

BAD LANDS BIGHORN

LESSER KONA FINCH

HEATH HEN

LER'S SEA COW

EASTERN ELK

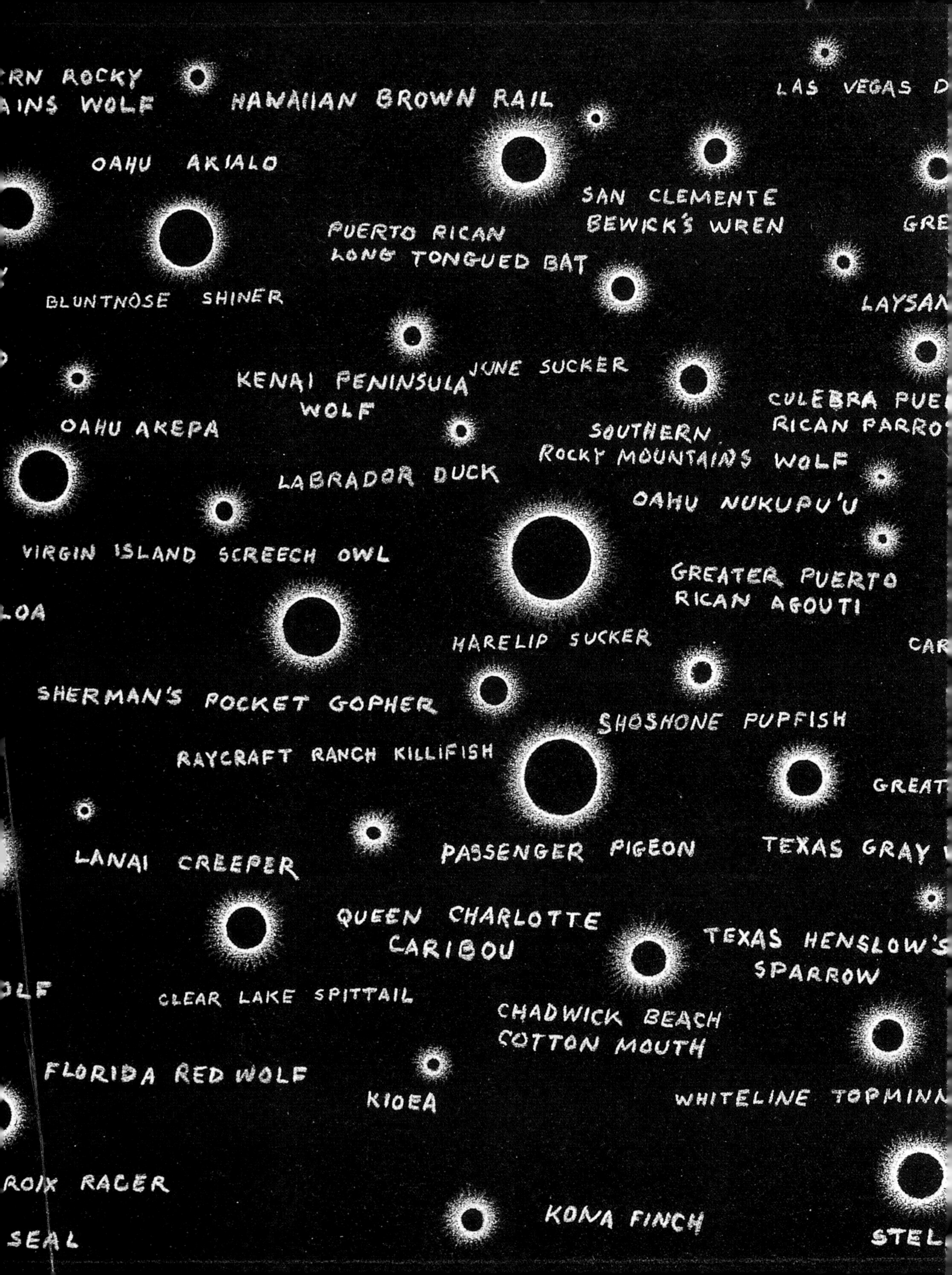

RN ROCKY
AINS WOLF
HAWAIIAN BROWN RAIL

LAS VEGAS D

OAHU AKIALO

SAN CLEMENTE
BEWICK'S WREN

GRE

PUERTO RICAN
LONG TONGUED BAT

BLUNTNOSE SHINER

LAYSAN

KENAI PENINSULA
WOLF

JUNE SUCKER

CULEBRA PUE
RICAN PARRO

OAHU AKEPA

SOUTHERN
ROCKY MOUNTAINS WOLF

LABRADOR DUCK

OAHU NUKUPU'U

VIRGIN ISLAND SCREECH OWL

GREATER PUERTO
RICAN AGOUTI

LOA

HARELIP SUCKER

CAR

SHERMAN'S POCKET GOPHER

SHOSHONE PUPFISH

RAYCRAFT RANCH KILLIFISH

GREAT

LANAI CREEPER

PASSENGER PIGEON

TEXAS GRAY

QUEEN CHARLOTTE
CARIBOU

TEXAS HENSLOW'S
SPARROW

LF

CLEAR LAKE SPITTAIL

CHADWICK BEACH
COTTON MOUTH

FLORIDA RED WOLF

KIOEA

WHITELINE TOPMINN

ROIX RACER

KONA FINCH

SEAL

STEL

Appendix II: Gatefold

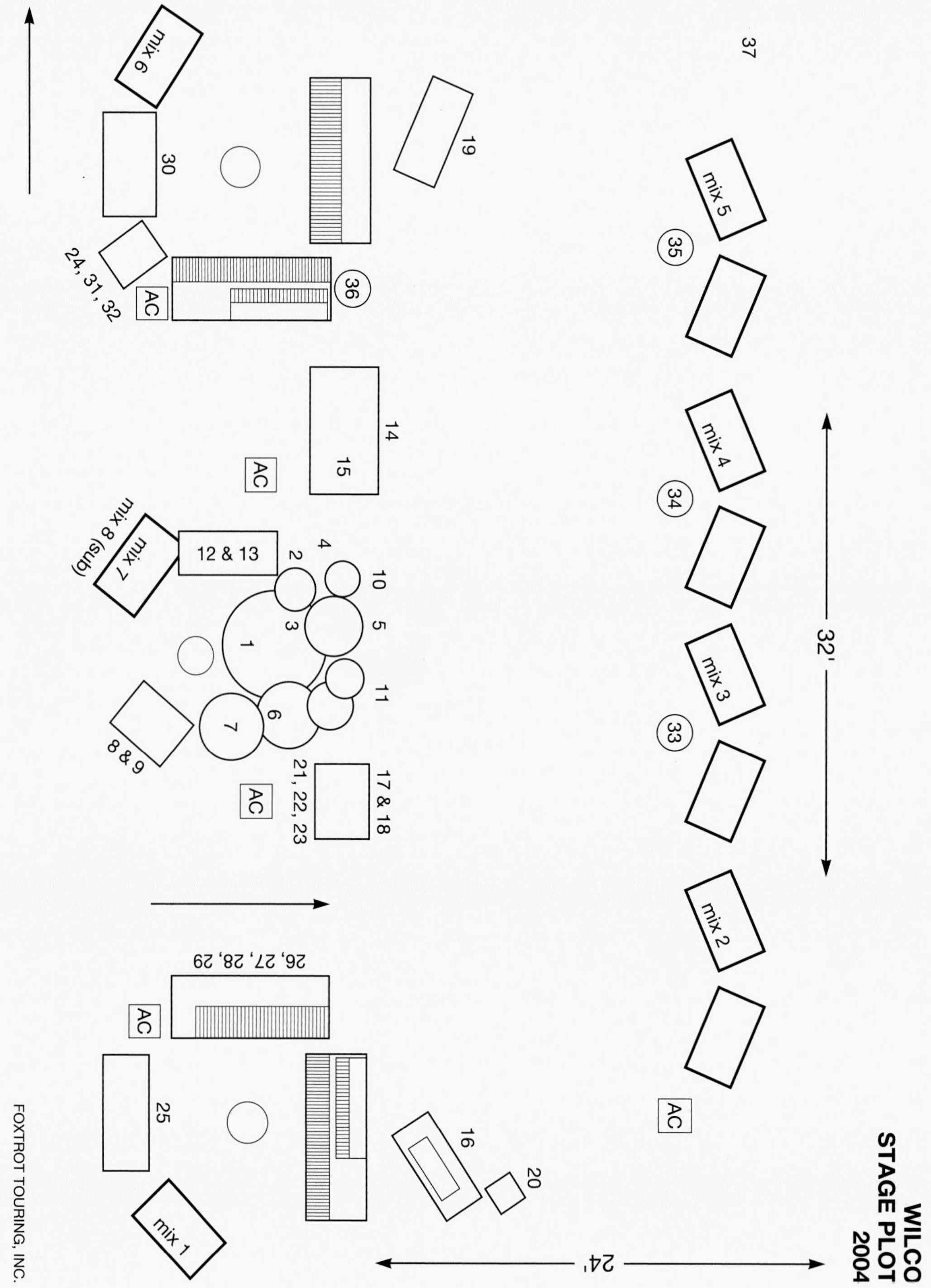

mix 6

30

24, 31, 32

AC

36

19

37

mix 5

35

mix 4

34

mix 3

33

32'

mix 2

AC

14

15

AC

mix 8 (sub)

mix 7

12 & 13

2

4

10

3

1

5

11

8 & 9

6

7

AC

21, 22, 23

17 & 18

26, 27, 28, 29

AC

25

16

20

mix 1

24'

FOXTROT TOURING, INC.

**WILCO
STAGE PLOT
2004**

(Inside) Fred Tomaselli, *Every Band I Can Remember Seeing, Every Vertebrae That Has Become Extinct Since 1492* (detail)

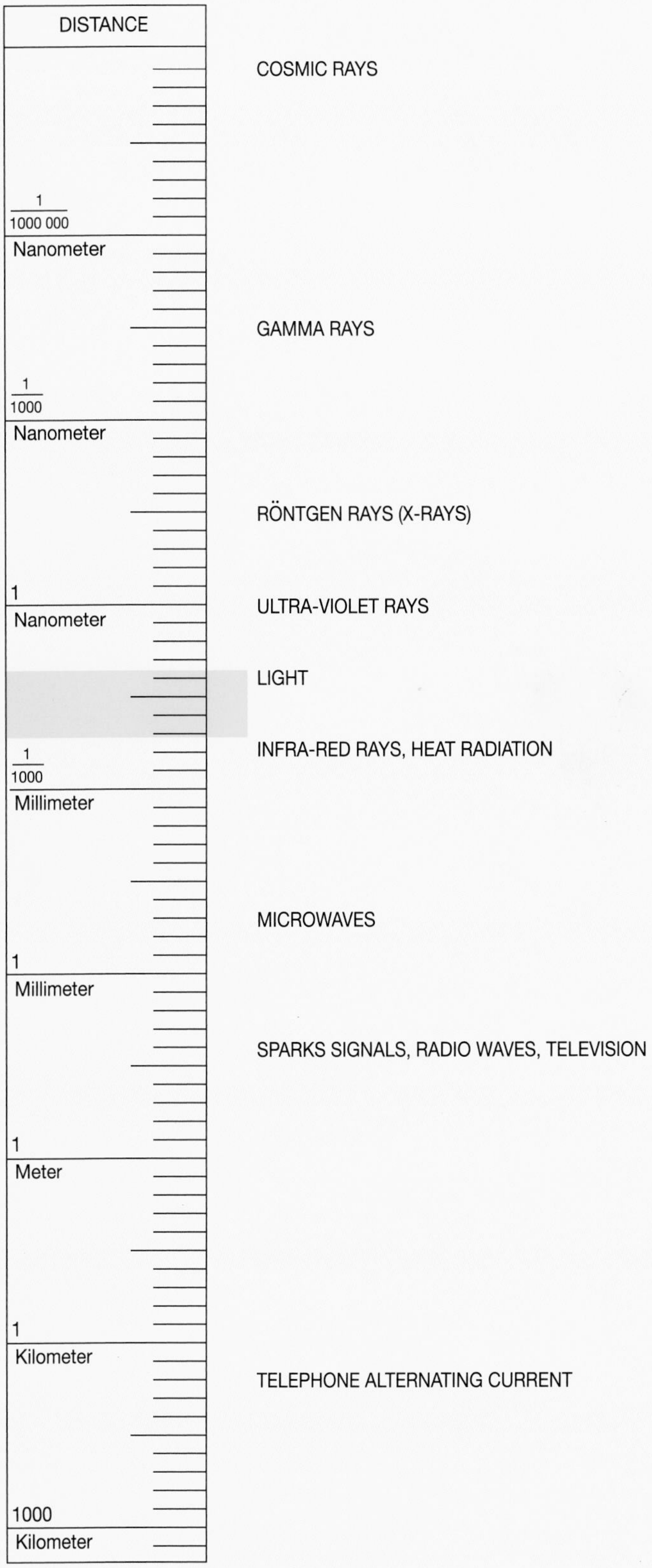

DISTANCE

COSMIC RAYS

$\dfrac{1}{1\,000\,000}$
Nanometer

GAMMA RAYS

$\dfrac{1}{1000}$
Nanometer

RÖNTGEN RAYS (X-RAYS)

1
Nanometer

ULTRA-VIOLET RAYS

LIGHT

$\dfrac{1}{1000}$
Millimeter

INFRA-RED RAYS, HEAT RADIATION

1
Millimeter

MICROWAVES

1
Meter

SPARKS SIGNALS, RADIO WAVES, TELEVISION

1
Kilometer

TELEPHONE ALTERNATING CURRENT

1000
Kilometer

RDINAIRES   PIXIES   MINOR THREAT

CHANNEL 3   OINGO BOINGO

THE GOGOS   THE PARTY BOYS   BOX BOYS   JAMAL DE

SUBURBAN LAWNS   ROBIN HITCHCOCK   DWINDLE FA

NEW RIDERS OF   MIDDLE
THE PURPLE SAGE   PHRANC   CLASS   THE

MOTHERS OF INVENTION   ALICE COOPER

ZOLAR X   DOOBIE BROS   THE MINUTE MEN

STETSON   AGENT ORANG

HOT TUNA   MARIA MULDAUR   BLACK FLAG
                                       MINIMAL   BUSTER P
IGGY + THE STOOGES   JO JO   MAN
                             GUN
                    GENESIS   FAT + FUCKED UP

VASSER   TRANQUILITY   THE CROWD   TH
CLEMENS
                                                                 LEONARD
                                                                  COHE
        DEAD KENNEDYS
                              THE FLY BOYS   CRAIG GRADY

EY CLARK   RAIN   BLURT
                                                   PARADE
        IMPOSTERS   ROXY MUSIC   BENT

                    THELONIUS   CHRISTMAS   HUMAN HAN
                    MONSTER
N'S CAR   CIRCLE JERKS   HARMONICA FATS   GEZA
                                                               MO
                          THE 3 O'CLOCK

        T.S.O.L   RANK + FILE
                        THE EYES
DY   54-40   BUTTHOLE

        MEAT   GREEN ON RED   WHITEHOUSE
        PUPPETS
                           THE HESITATIONS SACCHARIN   33   T
CS   TRUST   PYGMIES
                    SALVATION
                    ARMY   ANGELIC UPSTARTS

ARK STEWART   NICK CAVE + THE BAD

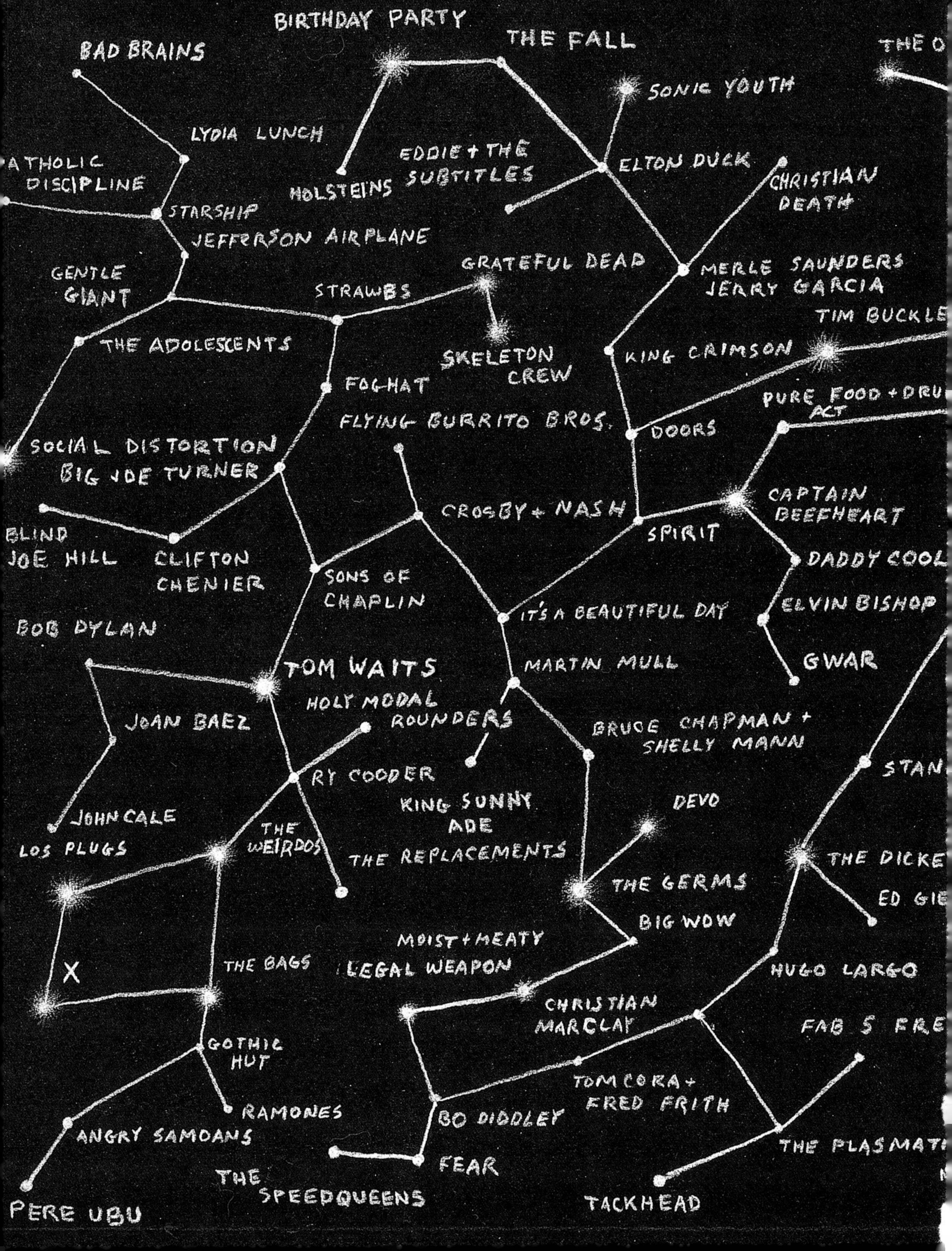

BIRTHDAY PARTY

THE FALL

THE O

BAD BRAINS

SONIC YOUTH

LYDIA LUNCH

EDDIE + THE
SUBTITLES

ELTON DUCK

CHRISTIAN
DEATH

ATHOLIC
DISCIPLINE

HOLSTEINS

STARSHIP

JEFFERSON AIRPLANE

GRATEFUL DEAD

MERLE SAUNDERS
JERRY GARCIA

TIM BUCKLE

GENTLE
GIANT

STRAWBS

SKELETON
CREW

KING CRIMSON

THE ADOLESCENTS

FOGHAT

PURE FOOD + DRU
ACT

FLYING BURRITO BROS.

DOORS

SOCIAL DISTORTION
BIG JOE TURNER

CROSBY + NASH

CAPTAIN
BEEFHEART

BLIND
JOE HILL

CLIFTON
CHENIER

SPIRIT

DADDY COOL

SONS OF
CHAPLIN

IT'S A BEAUTIFUL DAY

ELVIN BISHOP

BOB DYLAN

MARTIN MULL

GWAR

TOM WAITS

HOLY MODAL
ROUNDERS

BRUCE CHAPMAN +
SHELLY MANN

JOAN BAEZ

STAN

RY COODER

KING SUNNY
ADE

DEVO

JOHN CALE

THE
WEIRDOS

THE REPLACEMENTS

THE DICKE

LOS PLUGS

THE GERMS

ED GIE

X

BIG WOW

MOIST + MEATY

HUGO LARGO

THE BAGS

LEGAL WEAPON

CHRISTIAN
MARCLAY

FAB 5 FRE

GOTHIC
HUT

TOM CORA +
FRED FRITH

RAMONES

BO DIDDLEY

ANGRY SAMOANS

THE PLASMATI

THE
SPEEDQUEENS

FEAR

TACKHEAD

PERE UBU

Appendix III: Inglenntions

These drawings by Glenn Kotche depict as yet unbuilt drumming devices, dubbed "Inglenntions" by Jeff Tweedy. Some of Glenn's descriptions—"pressure devices," "chambers of chains"—wound up in the song "Wishful Thinking," when Glenn gave Jeff some copies of his idea notebooks in response to Jeff's request for lyric contributions from the rest of the band.

1. These are superball mallets—superballs, cut in half and mounted on sticks. They create great moaning sounds when rubbed on drumheads. **2.** Moving plates with a fulcrum. **3.** A multi-textured, serrated cymbal cone for making scraping

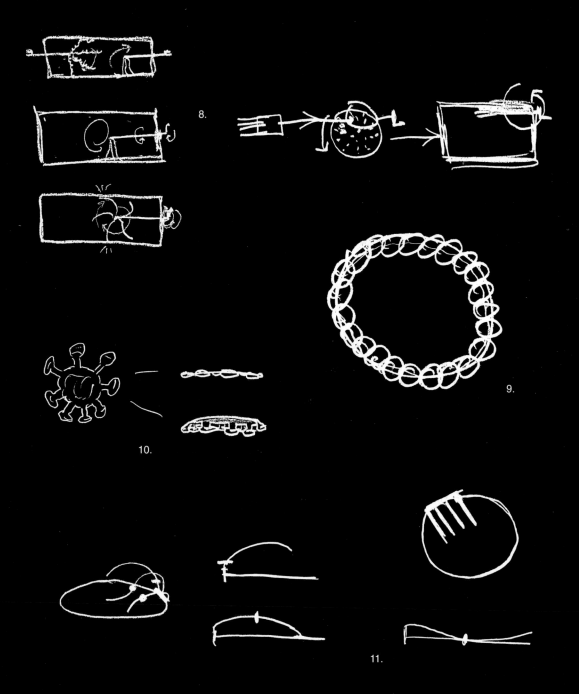

noises. **4.** Stacked metal plates. **5.** A chain drum. **6.** Three views of a spring chamber—springs stretched across a box. **7.** Some assorted prepared drumheads. **8.** A crank drum, consisting of a rod through the shell with chains, wires, or springs attached. The rod is rotated by hand to get a slow fan effect. **9.** Jingle bells. **10.** Bells. Attachments for a hi-hat. **11.** Weights that act as pressure devices on the drumheads for the attached preparations (wires, springs, chains, jingle bells, etc.).

Appendix IV: Walter Sear Tells His Story

I was born in April 1930. My father was a mechanical engineer—I grew up with tools in my hands. I always had a curiosity about electronics, and I began building things when I was eleven or twelve. I was especially interested in chemistry. I left home at fifteen, and worked my way through Temple University playing the tuba. I maintained an athletic scholarship as long as I showed up on Saturdays to play in the football band.

I became known in the Philadelphia area, especially in the Italian community, and eventually I would spend my summers playing the Italian Feast circuit up and down the Eastern Seaboard. The nice thing about that was that the Italian women in the neighborhood would cook for us, all showing off for the band. Part of being a musician is always knowing where the food is. In the studio, too—always know where the food is. The first thing I teach my assistants is: *Never order a hot meal in the studio, because by the time you get to that hamburger, it ll be cold, solidified grease.*

Eventually I went to The Curtis Institute of Music, and then into the Philadelphia Orchestra, where I remained a short time until enlisting in the U.S. Air Force, otherwise I would have been drafted and sent to Korea. I was accepted into the U.S. Air Force Band in Washington, where I was primarily an arranger, which left me so much free time that I immediately went back to school at the government's expense and got a master's degree in composition. All through this time, I was building things. It seemed inevitable that I'd combine science (especially physics) and music; they're intertwined. Going to the Wilco concert at Irving Plaza, for example—I enjoyed the music, but the brain doesn't stop working: I wondered why they were using ultra-subwoofers that go down below 52 hertz. The lowest musical note that you can get is 52 hertz, so why do you need a 20-hertz signal? It's an earthquake frequency—structurally, it's dangerous.

My first studio was opened in 1964 because of my friendship with Bob Moog. At the time I was working in the Radio City Music Hall Orchestra. There were four shows a day with a movie interspersed between each one, so every day I'd have six hours to kill. So you can either join the perpetual poker game that is still going on; you can chase 16-year-old Rockettes—and the divorce rate in the orchestra was *wow*—you're spending sixteen hours a day, three meals a day with these kids who are fresh off the farm; or you can do something constructive, which for me was to work on building theremins, which are the oldest electronic instrument and a long-standing interest of mine. I began to get called to do theremin dates around town, which I am still doing. I also started my own tuba-manufacturing business and have built around two thousand tubas.

I sold theremins for Moog. And then The Beatles came along, and everyone wanted to play electric guitar. The Japanese manufactured cheap electric guitars in bulk, but the problem was that amplifiers were too large, and thus too expensive, for cost-effective shipping. So Bob and I began manufacturing cheap amplifiers and jobbing them out to music dealers who would package them with the guitars and sell them as a kit. It was a disaster, of course—because any business enterprise we got into was a disaster.

Around this time we became interested in the synthesizer, and eventually Bob invented the Moog synthesizer. I bought the very first one and also sold them to various

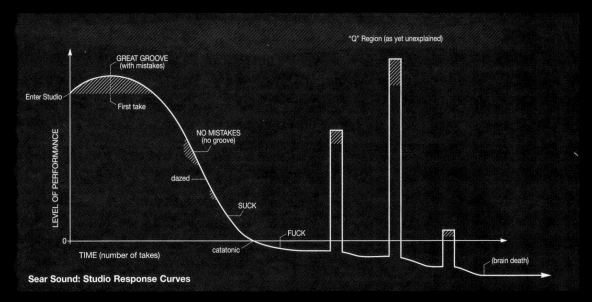

Sear Sound: Studio Response Curves

Labels in figure: "Q" Region (as yet unexplained); GREAT GROOVE (with mistakes); Enter Studio; First take; NO MISTAKES (no groove); dazed; SUCK; FUCK; catatonic; (brain death); LEVEL OF PERFORMANCE; TIME (number of takes); 0

music houses around town because it was a new and different sound. In the meantime, I'd opened up a showroom to sell synthesizers. And I was subletting a studio from Bob Fine, who ran a great recording studio called Fine Recording. Fine was one of the greatest engineers to walk the face of the earth. All this time I was also playing theremin and synthesizer at sessions all over New York, including the first uses of the synthesizer on a pop record (Simon & Garfunkel's *Bookends*) and in a commercial film (*Midnight Cowboy*).

In 1969 Bob Fine went out of business. He went broke because he was an inventive genius; he invented the fax machine, but with a different system, using shades of gray related to pitch. He put a lot of money into it, and he went broke, and the idea died for many years. I bought most of his assets and opened my own studio with his chief engineer in the Paramount Hotel building on 46th and Broadway in 1970. I took some session work and also did some low-budget film mixing for X-rated movies. The sound had to be mixed! And the studio did quite well.

I've never spent a dime on advertising, but people keep coming in. People like Sonic Youth, a group I almost destroyed because of my classical training. They came in the first night to record and I heard what was going on and I said *Hold on a minute, I'll be out to tune your guitars for you.* They said, "No!" We've been friends ever since. I gave them advice about building their home studio. When the Paramount Building was bought in 1988, we moved to 48th Street.

The philosophy of the studio is *listen to what you're doing, and make it sound as good as you can.* That's what most studios used to do. We spent a lot of time deciding what

equipment we would build and what was needed to make it sound better.

When Wilco wandered in, something happened. They felt it too. Most of the time, I go through my paces here, and it's okay. But when these guys came in I was excited, and I happen to like Jeff very much. And when their three-week stay became a three-month stay we got very close. The music was interesting, and they were trying to do something unique. And the talent and skill was unquestionably there. They used every piece of gear in the place, and experimented with things that you can't find anywhere else. Many things here sound different. We have about two hundred and fifty microphones, and they're all different.

But also, when thinking about music and designing equipment, appearance is fifty or sixty percent of it. If I have anything to say at all to Wilco, it's *Get a choreographer.* We're in showbiz, and you should never forget that. And for recording, things should look nice. If you look at all the microphones in this place, you won't see a scratch, a dent, or a piece of tape. Why? Because it's two inches in front of the singer's face. He's staring at this thing, and it should look nice. I was so surprised to see the egg on the Wilco cover. It's used a lot in the advertising industry. It's a perfect shape. Why do we eat chicken eggs instead of duck eggs? Because when a chicken lays an egg, she cackles, so we know when it's fresh. The duck eggs could've been sitting there all day. Got to cackle, got to advertise.

I still check in on all the sessions, and I'm the maintenance man here. Benjamin Franklin said, "Take care of your shop, and your shop will take care of you." I'm a great believer in that.

Appendix V: Credits

Henry Miller (1819–1980) lived in Brooklyn, Paris, and California. His books include *Tropic of Cancer*, *The Colossus of Maroussi*, and *The Rosy Crucifixion* trilogy.

Rick Moody is the author most recently of *Demonology* and *The Black Veil*.

PictureBox, Inc. is a New York-based visual-content studio and publishing house composed of Peter Buchanan-Smith and Dan Nadel. Peter is a former art director of the *New York Times* Op-Ed page, while Dan writes regularly for a variety of publications. Previous projects include *Speck* and *Fresh Dialogue Four*, both published by Princeton Architectural Press, as well as *Cheap Laffs: The Art of the Novelty Item*, for Harry N. Abrams, and the packaging design for Wilco's *A ghost is born*. Through its nonprofit wing, the studio also continues to produce the ongoing annual book of pictures and prose *The Ganzfeld* (*theganzfeld.com*) and other related projects.

Bern Porter's *Founds* (pictured in this book) have been considered a significant—if undervalued—achievement in American art. These poetic visual collages, crafted from magazine and advertisement clippings, draw on a body of work first explored by Marcel Duchamp's Readymades and Kurt Schwitters's *Merzbilder*. Porter completed several now out-of-print books of *Founds*, each thematically organized yet all related by their sardonic—though optimistic—critique of postwar American consumer culture.

Former physicist Porter (1911–2004), disturbed by his participation in the Manhattan Project, turned in the 1940s to what he considered constructive outlets for new technologies. Despite unending financial struggles, Porter immersed himself in a life of ideas; his achievements include: publishing ten books by and about Henry Miller, including an exhaustive bibliography of his work; managing a surrealist art gallery; participating in the international Mail Art phenomenon; and founding a so-called "think tank" for artists, The Institute of Advanced Thinking, in his native Maine. Collections of Porter's *Founds* and other work can be found at the University of California at Los Angeles Library, Brown University's John Hay Library, and in the Bern Porter Archive at the library of the Museum of Modern Art, New York.

Michael Schmelling's photographs have appeared in numerous national and international publications. A book of his photographs from El Paso, Texas, *Shut Up Truth*, was published in 2002 by J&L Books. He is represented by Wallspace Gallery. (*michaelschmelling.com*)

Fred Tomaselli's work has been shown in galleries and museums around the world. He is represented by James Cohan Gallery. His current studio, in Williamsburg, Brooklyn, is on the same street as Henry Miller's childhood home.

Formed in 1994, **Wilco** has released five records: *A.M.*; *Being There*; *Summerteeth*; *Yankee Hotel Foxtrot*; and, most recently, *A ghost is born*. Wilco has also collaborated with Billy Bragg (*Mermaid Avenue*, volumes I and II) and Minus 5 (*Down With Wilco*). Lyricist Jeff Tweedy has recently published a book of poetry, *Adult Head*, and teamed with drummer Glenn Kotche and collaborator Jim O'Rourke to form the band Loose Fur. Other projects include bassist John Stirratt's group The Autumn Defense and solo recordings from Kotche. Keyboardist Mikael Jorgensen joined the group in 2002. Currently based in Chicago, the lineup recently expanded to include multi-instrumentalist Pat Sansone and guitarist Nels Cline. They tour and record constantly.

A PICTUREBOX BOOK

Benefactors:
Nick Amster / Tony Margherita / Brian Taranto & Love Police

Music courtesy of Nonesuch Records

Editorial assistant: Jessi Rymill
Design assistant: Lindsay Ballant
Copy editor: Sarah Larson
Cover photo retoucher: Kathy Grove

Publicity: Deb Bernardini for Sacks & Co.

Thanks:
Nick Amster, Deb Bernardini, David Bither and Nonesuch Records, D.A.P., Ethan D'Ercole, T.J. Doherty, Isaac Green,
Josh Grier, Steven Guarnaccia, James Cohan Gallery, Deborah Johnson, Haydn Johnston, Robert Lemons,
Ben Levin, Mark Melnicove, Sue Miller, Matthew Nadel, Jim O'Rourke, Corey Rusk and Touch and Go,
Matthew Salacuse, Gregg Schaufeld, Bill and Abby Schmelling, Walter Sear,
Brian Taranto, Jason Tobias, Ken Waagner, Doug Wolske,
Amy Gray & Domenique Zuber

Found Poetry (Something Else Press, 1972) excerpted by permission of Bern Porter.

"The Angel Is My Watermark" by Henry Miller, from *Stand Still Like The Hummingbird*, copyright © 1962 by Henry Miller.
Reprinted by permission of New Directions Publishing Corp.

Fred Tomaselli images courtesy James Cohan Gallery.

10 9 8 7 6 5 4 3 2 1

PICTUREBOX, Inc.
228 West Houston Street, #3
New York, NY 10014
info@pictureboxinc.com | www.pictureboxinc.com

w w w . t h e w i l c o b o o k . c o m
w w w . w i l c o w o r l d . n e t

Appendix VI: Afterword

On June 8, 2004, a year after we began work on this book, Wilco returned to New York to play a warm-up concert for *A ghost is born*. With the departure of Leroy Bach and the addition of two new band members, Nels Cline and Pat Sansone, the band was suddenly a six-piece with an entirely new dynamic. We documented the show in order to bring the book full circle, one year and one album later, just a week away from the printing press. [PictureBox]

Nels Cline, guitar

Stan Doty, front of house engineer

Haydn Johnston, tour manager

Mikael Jorgensen, keyboards

Glenn Kotche, drums

Tony Margherita, manager

We used to play goodbye shows, but lately we've tried to use a special... It's a good tactic to leave people more excited. /151

Frankie Montuoro, guitar tech

Pat Sansone, multi-instrumentalist

John Stirratt, bass

Jason Tobias, production manager

Jeff Tweedy, guitar, vocals

Matt Zivich, stage tech

801	802	803	804	805	806	807	808	809	810
811	812	813	814	815	816	817	818	819	820
821	822	823	824	825	826	827	828	829	830
831	832	833	834	835	836	837	838	839	840
841	842	843	844	845	846	847	848	849	850
851	852	853	854	855	856	857	858	859	860
861	862	863	864	865	866	867	868	869	870
871	872	873	874	875	876	877	878	879	880
881	882	883	884	885	886	887	888	889	890
891	892	893	894	895	896	897	898	899	900
901	902	903	904	905	906	907	908	909	910
911	912	913	914	915	916	917	918	919	920
921	922	923	924	925	926	927	928	929	930
931	932	933	934	935	936	937	938	939	940
941	942	943	944	945	946	947	948	949	950
951	952	953	954	955	956	957	958	959	960
961	962	963	964	965	966	967	968	969	970
971	972	973	974	975	976	977	978	979	980
981	982	983	984	985	986	987	988	989	990
991	992	993	994	995	996	997	998	999	

(1000)

157

I Lift My Eyes Up to the Hills

White Cat New Life

Ixworth C.M.

Ps. 121: 1-8

Cotton Mather, 1718

Version of 1767

REINE LIEBE SUCHT NICHT SICH SELBER
LOVE THAT'S PURE, ITSELF DISDAINING

WO IST WOHL EIN SÜSSER LEBEN   8.7.8.7.6.6.6.7.7.

St. 3, 6, 8

Obituary

Zahn 6519

Johann A. Gruber, 1748
Sheema Z. Buehne, trans. 1965

Johann Balthasar König, 1738

We can outguess him, he longs for a poet, a candidate with depth   an attempt. If angst had ability.

Look! A young man just a baby Not even a splash! lipsynching a life,   it moves!

expects cash he worries for support he learns to crawl on blades! most people cringe but he works no red snarls!

Back at the funeral home
and his crisis to memorize
he retreats from
the question,
worries for the bartender
begs for an event. weeps over easy developments
breathes
televisions, and
far from his sea
a poisonous spider
steals from his bartender,
a brokenhearted ambition
his Heaven
that none
or most of us
too many of us
are not enough of them
only
his television suffers

159

JOYFULLY, JOYFULLY   10.10.10.10.D.

St. 1-3

Old Maid

William Hunter, 1843

Abraham Down Merrill, 1845

I think we're gett - ing old, Gal, my heart's grown colder, your hair is turning gray,

so come on what do you say, let's put the horse behind the cart and make some hay

Old maid,   we're not getting any younger,   this old way, of counting your chickens when you get   laid.

I know you two were best of friends
because she's the one you let in
well she's dead and that's a fact
and what I'm getting at...
I was just hoping we could do better than that

Now you know it's not a sin
and I've known you since way back when
never in the month of May,
June, August or September
but how about today
Old Maid!

160

THE WORLD, THE DEVIL, AND TOM PAINE   COME AND GO ALONG WITH ME   L.M.

St. 1-3   Shadowless

Anon., 1807   Anon., 1868

white hot beehive   She wants to die like people do

shower insect-clicking summer was sickening in that room   high in the heat

a white hot beehive
she was doomed
she has a wing proferred to the sky
she couldn't stop sinking,
though she wasn't thinking
she wanted to night fly
she wants to live
Like people do

A circuit rider

161

I Have Fought the Good Fight

THE DEATH SONG 12.12.12.12.

St. 1-6

My Words

Jared B. Waterbury, 1831

Anon., 1831

I have a mouth for the wind and a circle of words that get lost,   toil disabled, blow like a bag down the alley,

tilt backwards up the staircase,   roll across traffic, sleep naked, throw themselves off fire escapes

how warm my words as the telephone sweats

you can feel how warm my words are.

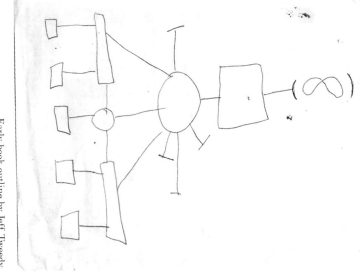

Early book outline by Jeff Tweedy

This was a period of finding poetry of my own. I wanted order, which I appreciated. The orderliness of verse appealed to me—as it must to any man—but even more I wanted a new order. I was positively repelled by the old order which, to me, amounted to restriction.

—William Carlos Williams, *I Wanted to Write a Poem*